Advertising Rights
The Neglected Freedom
Toward a New Doctrine of Commercial Speech

Advertising Rights The Neglected Freedom

TOWARD A NEW DOCTRINE OF COMMERCIAL SPEECH

Richard T. Kaplar

WITH AN INTRODUCTION BY
Harvey L. Zuckman

Media Policy Series

the media institute

Washington, D.C.

Table of Contents

Preface

About halfway through its now 12-year history, The Media Institute ran head on into what we felt (and still feel) was a major problem: the lack of any proper application of the First Amendment to those "structural" policies (the laws and regulations) that hold sway over the business activities of media and communications companies.

Among the kinds of things that have troubled us, and that we have addressed over the years, are the extraordinary degree of local government control over cable TV companies; the FCC's ban on network syndication of entertainment programs; the governmental hurdles standing in the way of the development of remote sensing technology for the news media; the ban on the entry of the Baby Bells into the information services business; and numerous appendages (including the Fairness Doctrine) of the so-called "public interest" standard.

To date, our record in these matters is hard to calculate because, for the most part, they are still pending. But one thing is clear and constant—now, as from the beginning, advocates of the linkage between the First Amendment and these structural policies are few and far between. With some rare (if noteworthy) exceptions, most legal scholars, First Amendment activists, and even First Amendment "practitioners" (*i.e.*, journalists) tend to neglect, or even reject, the notion that the First Amendment applies here too.

I am reminded of this history as, with the publication of this book, the Institute embarks on yet another campaign: full application of the First Amendment to commercial speech. As Yogi Berra said, it feels like *deja vu* all over again. Indeed, the attitude of most people (including First Amendment advocates) to advertisers' claims of First Amendment rights can be likened to the attitude shown the estranged and somewhat disreputable relative who, uninvited, nevertheless shows up at the wedding: Nobody knows him very well, they're not entirely sure what to do with him, and, truth be told, they're a little embarrassed that he's there at all.

So why are we doing this? The short answer is because our values, and no less importantly our *experience*, leave us no choice.

During the last five or six years, we at The Media Institute have come to believe, because we've seen them firsthand, things that are sometimes dismissed as cliches or generalities.

Among the most salient: (1) But for an independent judiciary, the First Amendment, and indeed the whole of the Bill of Rights, would not be worth the paper it is printed on. This, because regulators and legislators, in their rush to make policies, neither know nor care enough about constitutional rights; (2) the majesty of an independent judiciary notwithstanding, much of the Supreme Court's First Amendment case law and dicta is contradictory and incomplete; and (3) the First Amendment is not divisible. Weaken it in its application in one area, and you weaken it *as a whole*.

Through numerous court and regulatory actions of which we've been a part, we are persuaded that there is a direct-line relationship between many structural laws and regulations, on the one hand, and the practice of journalism on the other. Moreover, we see in these structural policies other kinds of injury to the First Amendment even where they don't have a direct impact on journalism.

Such is our mindset and our experience as we now approach the subject of commercial speech, and thus do we reject totally the comfortable and somewhat smug argument advanced by those who claim that restrictions placed on commercial speech (no matter what they may be) will not affect political speech. In the first place, we don't share their confidence. And second, commercial speech is speech, and deserving of First Amendment guarantees in its own right. At a bare minimum we are certain that it is impossible to strip some commercial speech (or speakers) of First Amendment protection without gravely imperiling the rest.

Over the course of the next few months, and years, we intend to give commercial speech activities a prominent place in our affairs. In addition to publications and conferences, we hope to file motions and comments with regulatory agencies, and *amicus* and intervenor briefs in the courts.

This book, however, represents the first and quite possibly best chance we will have to speak to, and (we hope) to recruit, a broad-based audience. If, after reading it, anyone is moved to want to carry a spear in this army, let us hear from you. We're looking for all the help we can get.

Patrick D. Maines
President
The Media Institute
March 1991

Introduction

Harvey L. Zuckman

This may be the most important book ever published on commercial speech and the First Amendment because it sounds the alarm as never before that this form of expression is in grave peril of governmental subjugation. It is must reading for everyone who believes in the free expression of truthful information without any "ifs, ands, or buts."

The author reviews the checkered history of the commercial speech doctrine from the time almost 50 years ago when the Supreme Court in an off-handed opinion declared commercial speech to be beyond the pale of constitutional protection. He notes the Court's almost complete change of heart and its extension of substantial First Amendment protection to even simple "buy and sell" proposals in the mid-1970s. But, alas, that was the high-water mark for commercial speech protection and, as the author details, it has been downhill ever since. Today, freedom of commercial speech is in serious jeopardy from well-intentioned but misguided judges, legislators, administrative officials, and assorted saviors of the world.

The author sounds the clarion call to battle to defend what remains of First Amendment protection and to roll back recent unwise and unconstitutional limitations on commercial speech. He does this first by delineating as no one has done so clearly before the reasons for the Supreme Court's erosion of constitutional protection in recent years. First is the Court's embrace, without historical support or sound policy basis, of the theory of a hierarchy of First Amendment values with political speech at the top of the scale and commercial speech near the bottom, resting just above indecent adult expression.

Until very recently neither Supreme Court decisions nor language recognized any hierarchy of First Amendment protection. There is certainly nothing in the history of the Amendment that justifies different treatment for different forms of protected expression. It will not wash historically to say that commercial speech was not significant in the life of early post-revolutionary America when the Bill of Rights was drafted. It was present in abundance and the drafters simply did not exclude such expression from First Amendment protection.

Worse yet, the Supreme Court's refusal to recognize the reality that free expression is a seamless web requiring across-the-board protection is dangerous social policy that threatens the very expression which the Court places at the top of its hierarchy—political speech. That seamlessness is illustrated by the Court's own recent and unfortunate decision in *Austin v. Michigan Chamber of Commerce*, 110 S. Ct. 1391 (1990), upholding state regulation preventing incorporated trade associations from buying, independently, newspaper advertisements on behalf of candidates for political office. Here, the present Court's zeal for undoing constitutional safeguards for commercial speech results in a weakening of protection for political expression as well.

As Justice Kennedy says in his dissent: "The other censorship scheme, I most regret to say, is of our own creation. It is value-laden, content-based speech suppression that permits some nonprofit corporate groups but not others to engage in political speech. After failing to disguise its animosity and distrust for the particular kind of political speech here at issue—the qualifications of a candidate to understand economic matters—the Court adopts a rule that allows Michigan to stifle the voices of some of the most respected groups in public life, on subjects central to the integrity of our democratic system." *Id.* at 1416-1417.

Even were we to concede that free expression is not a seamless web, commercial speech is of such overarching value to our society that judges and legislators ought to be following the author's prescription to strengthen and not weaken constitutional protection. As Justice Brennan so insightfully pointed out in his dissenting opinion in *Dun & Bradstreet, Inc. v. Greenmoss Builders, Inc.*, 472 U.S. 749, 787-788 (1985): "Speech about commercial or economic matters, even if not directly implicating 'the central meaning of the First Amendment,'. . . is an important part of our public discourse. . . . [T]he choices we make when we step into the voting booth may well be the products of what we have learned from the myriad of daily economic and social phenomenon [sic] that surround us." The consequences for a free society from our elected and appointed officials not understanding this may be both unfortunate and profound. Mr. Kaplar's book contributes significantly to that critical understanding and shapes the debate for the better.

The second reason for the erosion of protection identified by the author is the Rehnquist Court's unprincipled willingness to change the rules of First Amendment protection when it doesn't approve of the particular commercial speech involved. As the author puts it, "the rules by which the balancing game is played can be changed from case to case at the whim of the Court. . . ."

Perhaps the chief significance of this work lies not in its detailing of the Supreme Court's erroneous legal analysis but in its identification of the factors at work creating the judicial mendacity toward affording First Amendment protection to commercial speech. For once these factors are identified it becomes possible to mount an effective counterattack. According to the author they include the mistaken notion that commercial speech is more easily verifiable and durable (and therefore easier to regulate than political speech) and, further, the failure of the Court and other proponents of regulation to define what it is they are permitting to be regulated.

The definitional problem lies at the heart of the Court's recent misguided efforts to deal with commercial speech; the author performs a valuable service in developing a definition of commercial speech that justifies full First Amendment protection for "truthful speech about lawful products and activities. . . ."

He further provides us with what I believe to be a workable six-point plan to ensure that the First Amendment rights of the audience for commercial expression are properly protected. My only reservation regarding the plan is that the author does not push his fifth point far enough. This point is to remind the Congress and the state legislatures that they have an obligation to act in accord with the Constitution. I would include under this point state and federal judges and would-be judges as well. I would urge that those concerned by the present erosion of commercial speech protection be prepared to send a message by challenging future judicial nominees to express their views on the First Amendment as it applies to commercial expression as well as to political speech, and to oppose the appointment or election of those who are ambivalent or negative toward constitutional protection for the former.

There are two details of Mr. Kaplar's manifesto with which I am in disagreement. First, I believe he is wrong to include proposed limitations on the amount of time available for commercials on children's television programs within the category of impermissible regulation of commercial speech. It seems to me that such regulation may be constitutionally justified as an appropriate time, place, or manner restriction on expression. In addition, such limitation is justified by the psychological vulnerability of the audience to commercial suggestion and is analogous to the less-exacting constitutional limitations approved by the Supreme Court for the suppression of child pornography in contrast to standards imposed for suppressing adult obscenity.

Second, I do not share his skepticism about the solution embraced recently by the voters of California: a scheme involving increased taxation of cigarette consumption, the proceeds of which are to be used in part to fund anti-smoking advertising campaigns. Without such a scheme the opponents of tobacco consumption would not be able to reach the same audience for tobacco advertising about whose right to information Mr. Kaplar is justifiably concerned. A.J. Liebling's cynical but rather accurate dictum that freedom of the press belongs to he who owns one is undermined by the California referendum scheme and permits access to a mass audience even by those who do not own a press (or a television station). The proper corrective for commercial speech that some perceive as abhorrent (such as tobacco advertising) is *more speech* that reaches the mass marketplace with a contrasting message. It is certainly not, as the author correctly argues elsewhere, *more regulation*.

Aside from these few details I fully subscribe to the statement of the nature of the danger to freedom of commercial speech outlined in this book, and the battle plan suggested by the author to preserve this important freedom and other freedoms linked to it.

As I said at the outset, this is an important book that has great meaning for everyone who cares about freedom of speech, freedom of the press, and, yes, even freedom of contract in our democratic free-market society.

I. Threats to a Fragile Freedom

"The greatest dangers to liberty lurk in insidious encroach-
ment by men of zeal, well-meaning but without understanding."

—Justice Louis D. Brandeis[1]

Commercial speech, or what most of us think of as advertising,
enjoys a prominent and well-established place in society that stretches
back to the colonial era. Few people should be surprised or even
alarmed at this since we live in a free-market economy that is driven
by the economic choices of information-seeking consumers. But advertising has hardly been afforded the same prominence in constitutional
circles, where it has been forced to languish in perpetual second-class
status. As a form of expression, commercial speech has received
amounts of First Amendment protection ranging from zero to something less than 100 percent, but has never been granted total protection from government interference. (And we are speaking here, as
we will throughout this book, only of truthful speech about lawful

1

products and services—not about false or misleading advertising which falls outside of First Amendment protection altogether.)

Currently commercial speech enjoys some degree of protection, but its future in this regard is uncertain and possibly even perilous. Today advertising is being threatened by a confluence of circumstances involving the courts, Congress, federal and state regulators, and perhaps most importantly public attitudes, all of which are coming together in a way that is unique—and uniquely harmful—in the history of commercial speech.

Oddly enough, this form of expression has suffered as much at the hands of those who practice a sort of benign neglect as from those who actively oppose its full protection. The ranks of staunch First Amendment defenders are heavily populated with lawyers and legal scholars who are not active in promoting commercial speech rights, or who themselves believe commercial speech is a backwater of First Amendment jurisprudence, or who just choose to ignore the topic. The American public, meanwhile, is largely uninformed about (and apparently uninterested in) the constitutional implications of restricting this one variety of speech. The indifference of both scholars and the public is regrettable though less understandable in the case of the former. After all, a threat to one type of speech becomes a threat to all speech—and to the very concept of freedom of speech embodied in the First Amendment.

Out of Balance

The system of checks and balances among legislators, regulators, and the courts that worked reasonably well at protecting commercial speech for the past 15 years has been thrown out of balance—and may fail entirely when next tested. Historically the system has worked something like this: Members of Congress, in well-meaning attempts to protect consumers from themselves, introduce bills aimed at reducing the consumption of disfavored products. The Federal Trade Commission (FTC), animated by a similar zeitgeist, proposes regulations toward the same end. These federal bodies are joined by state legislatures and attorneys general who attempt to legislate and regulate consumer behavior within their own borders. Proposals to reduce consumption of disfavored products typically include provisions to greatly restrict or ban altogether the advertising of those products. Alcohol beverages and tobacco products have been the most consistently disfavored, and consequently their advertising has been the most heavily regulated. In 1990 alone, for example, bills introduced in Congress would have gone far beyond restrictions already in place and would have effectively banned most if not all advertising for alcohol and tobacco. But these products are hardly alone—advertising restrictions have been proposed for a host of other legal products including foods making health claims, presweetened cereals, airline tickets, and products advertised on children's TV shows.

The opportunities for legislative and regulatory mischief are almost endless, since it is possible to imagine one ill effect or another for virtually any product. In their zeal to restrict even truthful advertising, however, lawmakers and regulators consistently fail to realize that their proposed restrictions on speech have serious constitutional implications. This is where the courts, and the U.S. Supreme Court in particular, have traditionally been counted on to provide a critical check in defense of the First Amendment. In 1976 the Supreme Court recognized the protected nature of commercial speech, and in 1980 articulated a four-part test to limit restrictions on truthful advertising.[2] These actions seemed to make it clear that outlandish legislative and regulatory schemes would not withstand constitutional scrutiny. As a result, few such proposals became law or regulation, and those that did quickly faced court challenges. The system was working, more or less, and the First Amendment was holding its own.

But Court decisions in recent years have dangerously weakened this First Amendment check. In 1986 the Court said in *Posadas de Puerto Rico Associates v. Tourism Company of Puerto Rico*[3] that the state could ban the advertising of any product, provided the state had the authority to ban the product itself. In essence it said that a company's right to speak about a product was no greater than its right to produce and sell the product. And in *S.U.N.Y. v. Fox*,[4] the Court in 1989 weakened its four-part test to say that an advertising restriction must only be a *reasonable* means—and no longer necessarily the *least restrictive* means—of advancing the government's interest.

Thus a new dynamic has been created, and we need not stretch our imagination to envision the consequences if *Posadas* and *S.U.N.Y.* are strictly interpreted in the future: The government may, at any time, find reasons to ban lots of products and services, and the result under *Posadas* might well be wholesale bans on the advertising for those products and services. Short of outright bans, whatever regulations are imposed need not be the least restrictive on speech but merely "reasonable" under *S.U.N.Y.*, however loosely that may be defined.

The practical effect: Legislative and regulatory proposals once deemed outlandish may suddenly become constitutional, and we may see a wave of regulations crashing down on truthful advertising for legal products and services as we have not seen before. The Court has made its check on First Amendment protection for commercial speech more uncertain, and future levels of protection for advertising across the board have become more unpredictable. If the struggle to protect the First Amendment can be thought of as an ongoing drama, the Court may have set the stage for some most disconcerting if not downright tragic scenes.

Unfortunately, a large portion of the audience (*i.e.*, the public) is likely to react by applauding these developments; perhaps the best we can hope for is unbridled indifference. What is it about the First Amendment that would provoke such a reaction? Actually we are not witnessing a groundswell of opposition to free speech *per se*; no doubt most of those who favor ad bans on disfavored products would claim to be staunch supporters of the First Amendment. Rather, we are seeing what results when the First Amendment happens to get in the way of popularly held values on other topics, especially where those topics are perceived to be problems that can be solved with a dose of good old American pragmatism.

Smoking and alcohol abuse, of course, have been targeted as public-health problems for some time. Levels of cholesterol, salt, and sugar consumption have been cited more recently as trouble spots. Since problem solving tends to be a pragmatic endeavor, it is usually more concerned with ends (the solution) than with means. In the case of smoking and drinking the reduction of consumption can be sought through various means—setting minimum ages for purchase and use; restricting the settings where the products may or may not be used; imposing legal penalties for misuse (in the case of alcohol); imposing prohibitive taxes; restricting or banning advertising of the products (although a significant body of evidence suggests this is not effective)—or, in the extreme, banning the manufacture and sale of the offending products altogether. Pragmatists who would like to see smoking and drinking levels reduced would argue that any and all such means are appropriate and should be employed aggressively. What the pragmatist overlooks, however, is that one of these means— advertising restrictions—happens to involve freedom of speech, a constitutionally protected right. As a value, freedom of speech aspires to be an absolute, above and apart from other values that can be bartered and traded off in pursuit of one social goal or another. But individuals (no matter how intelligent and well intentioned) who pursue otherwise commendable social goals do not wish to hear this; to make freedom of speech an absolute value is to place advertising restrictions out of bounds—and that is to deprive them of one more problem solving option. Meanwhile the public at large, confronted with the possibility of solving a troublesome social problem even if it means doing some unspecified damage to an abstract constitutional concept, is bound to choose pragmatically at the expense of principle.

This mindset is not limited to the man in the street, of course. Politicians and regulators are consummate pragmatists, as a sampling of their recent proposals will indicate. Unfortunately, they are more likely to be encouraged rather than restrained by the type of public attitude described above, and are now perhaps less likely to be tempered by the Court. A remarkable disregard for constitutional concerns can be discerned among the following examples of initiatives by Congress, regulatory agencies, and the states. These proposals would have the effect of restricting or even banning advertising in ways clearly inimical to the First Amendment.

United States Congress

Alcohol Advertising. A recent proposal to require five rotating warn-ing messages in all advertisements for alcoholic beverages embod-ied the type of paternalism that the Supreme Court had rejected 14 years earlier. The proposed legislation was introduced in 1990 by Sen. Albert Gore, Jr. (D-Tenn.) and Rep. Joseph Kennedy (D-Mass.) as S.2439 and H.R.4493. It required advertisers to include government-mandated messages of up to 34 words in print ads and spoken mes-sages of up to 21 words in television and radio ads; those broadcast warnings were to be presented "in an audible and deliberate manner and in a length of time that allows for a clear understanding. . . ." Critics were quick to point out that the Gore/Kennedy legislation would have the practical effect of eliminating most broadcast ads because the warn-ing message would consume too much of a 15- or 30-second spot. Fortunately this bill did not become law in the 101st Congress, but it is all too typical of legislative schemes to limit commercial speech for a variety of legal products in ways that are blatantly unconstitutional.

Tobacco Advertising. This restrictive trend is even more evident in the realm of tobacco advertising, which has been the subject of numerous and even more far-reaching schemes to squelch commer-cial speech. In 1989, for example, bills introduced in the House by Rep. Thomas A. Luken (D-Ohio) (H.R.1250) and Rep. Michael Synar (D-Okla.) (H.R.1493) would have reduced tobacco advertising to black-and-white "tombstone" ads with prominent warning messages. A similar bill (S.1883) was introduced in the Senate by Sen. Edward Kennedy (D-Mass.). A bill by Sen. Bill Bradley (D-N.J.) would have required that a warning about tobacco addiction be added to the four rotating warnings in use. Rep. James Slattery (D-Kans.)introduced a bill (H.R.1171) that would have required such a warning in addition to one of the rotating warnings. None of these bills became law.

In 1990 restrictions on tobacco advertising were focused in two bills, Sen. Kennedy's S.1883 and the "Tobacco Control and Health Pro-tection Act" (H.R.5041) by Rep. Henry A. Waxman (D-Cal.), a suc-cessor to the sweeping Luken bill (H.R.1250) and similar to the Kennedy measure. A brief look at this bill will demonstrate the lengths to which some members of Congress are willing to go in order to restrict or effectively ban tobacco advertising. H.R.5041 contained provisions that would have required that tobacco ads:

- Use no colors other than black and white to describe the product (*i.e.*, tombstone ads).
- Display no trademark logos or symbols.
- Portray no human or cartoon figures.
- Contain no pictures other than a single tobacco package.
- Double the number of warning messages and rotate them among ads.
- Devote at least 20 percent of the ad space to a magnified warning message.
- Print the message in black, white, and red (with the word "warning" in red) in a bordered box at the top of the ad.
- Display a second warning message in the tobacco package picture that takes up at least 25 percent of the picture.
- Include any additional information required by the Secretary of Health and Human Services.
- Adhere to additional restrictions that any state or locality may choose to impose.

Legislative proposals such as this do not seem to be mindful of the protections the Supreme Court has afforded commercial speech since the mid-1970s. Once again we are presented with bills such as Waxman's and Kennedy's that attempt to restrict truthful advertising of legal products (which the Court set as a threshold requirement for protecting commercial speech in 1980).

These particular bills also raised serious concerns because they would have permitted state and local governments to impose their own restrictions on tobacco advertising within their jurisdictions. Giving the green light to local regulation, and the thousands of additional ad restrictions this might spawn, was widely viewed as a not-so-covert attempt to ban tobacco advertising altogether, since advertisers could not hope to comply in a cost-effective way with a nationwide crazy quilt of regulation. At this writing no new tobacco ad restrictions have been passed by Congress, although the issue is not likely to go away.

Children's Advertising. In October 1990 Congress enacted legislation to restrict the amount of commercial time on children's programming. The law directs the Federal Communications Commission to promulgate rules limiting commercial time during children's programs to 10.5 minutes per hour on weekends and 12 minutes per hour on weekdays. The FCC was also directed to establish guidelines for identifying and regulating "program-length commercials."

Here again the actions of Congress raise serious constitutional questions. It is difficult to see how the government's stated interest of improving the quality and increasing the quantity of children's programming will be directly advanced by the legislation. Nor is it evident how restrictions on commercial time can be considered a "narrowly tailored," reasonable means of improving programming.

The legislation raises additional problems of definition. How the FCC defines "program-length commercial," for example, will have significant implications for whether programs will be treated as protected speech, or as commercial speech that is effectively banned from the air. (A 30-minute children's program deemed to be a "program-length commercial" would violate the 10.5- or 12-minute time restriction and thus be banned.) However, as the Supreme Court noted in a 1990 decision on lawyer advertising,[5] categories of advertising cannot be banned merely because they are potentially misleading. Nor would such a ban be a "narrowly tailored" remedy as contemplated in *S.U.N.Y.*

State Legislatures

State lawmakers have been no less fervent than their federal colleagues in wanting to restrict or ban advertising, especially for tobacco and alcohol. A look at state legislative activity for only one year (1990) reveals that a host of such measures were introduced, although none became law.

Attempting to ban outdoor advertising signs seemed to be a popular legislative pastime in 1990. Nine states, plus the cities of Chicago and Philadelphia, entertained measures to ban outdoor ads for alcohol and/or tobacco products, typically from areas in sight of elementary and secondary schools, parks and playgrounds, universities, or hospitals. Fourteen states considered bans or restrictions on other types of advertising for alcohol and/or tobacco. Legislation proposed in four states—New York, California, Florida, and Iowa—sought to eliminate the tax deductibility of advertising expenses for alcohol and/or tobacco products, and in New York State an additional tax on tobacco advertising was sought.

In related developments, the Washington State Liquor Control Board proposed a hopelessly overbroad regulation to ban ads "designed or intended to attract persons under the legal age of consumption to consume alcoholic beverages." The state legislature sparked to the idea, entertaining a bill to ban alcohol ads within the state, and a joint resolution urging the U.S. Congress to ban entirely or restrict the content of television ads for alcohol products. And in California, health officials undertook a costly if questionable $28.6-million anti-smoking advertising campaign financed by the state's excise tax on tobacco.

In New York City a proposed regulation would have required all disclosures in radio and television ads to be stated orally, and would have required minimum type sizes for disclosures in print ads. Several states, including Iowa, Maryland, Florida, and Nevada, considered or adopted restrictions on lawyer advertising.

Thus, as the 101st Congress and various state legislatures amply demonstrated, we cannot look to the legislative branch to foster (or even to comprehend, it would seem) the First Amendment rights for commercial speech articulated by the Supreme Court. This is unfortunate but perhaps not surprising since it is the nature of Congress and state legislatures, as political bodies, to function by being both reactive to problems and responsive to compromise. Neither characteristic has much to do with upholding principles (such as freedom of speech) for their own sake.

State Attorneys General

The regulation of advertising at the state level is carried out by state attorneys general. Spurred on by the National Association of Attorneys General, however, a number of attorneys general in recent years have become very aggressive in attempting to regulate national advertising within their states. From a First Amendment perspective this has proved unfortunate because these officials generally demonstrate little concern for commercial speech rights. Moreover, the regulations they impose are often more restrictive than federal regulations, not only burdening advertisers with multiple and conflicting requirements, but raising challenges to the federal government's preemption of authority to regulate national advertising.

In Iowa, for example, the Kellogg Company sued Iowa Attorney General Tom Miller to keep the state from restricting the company's ads. Kellogg stated in its suit that the state's action would violate federal statutes governing interstate commerce, advertising, and food labeling practices. Miller countersued, alleging that the Kellogg ads contained deceptive and misleading health claims. In contrast, the FTC had praised an earlier Kellogg advertising campaign for All Bran cereal which stated that "the National Cancer Institute believes a high-fiber, low-fat diet may reduce your risk of some kinds of cancer"; that the National Cancer Institute recommends eating high-fiber foods; and that, ounce for ounce, no food has more fiber than Kellogg's All Bran. The director of the FTC's Bureau of Consumer Protection called the ads "exactly the kind of adequately substantiated and responsible vehicles for providing beneficial information to the public that we believe it is important for regulatory programs to encourage, not discourage."[6] Should the consumers of Iowa be denied the "beneficial information" that is available to consumers in the other 49 states? The Quaker Oats Company has been engaged in a similar dispute with Attorney General Jim Mattox of Texas.

Attorney General Mattox had also attempted to assert state authority over the regulation of airline fare advertising. In *Trans World Airlines v. Mattox*,[7] however, the U.S. Court of Appeals for the Fifth Circuit held that the Texas state regulation was preempted by federal law, although the circumstances of the case limited the ruling to airline advertising. The Supreme Court subsequently refused to review the lower court's decision.

This new militance on the part of state attorneys general poses grave concerns for the First Amendment. The impulse to extend one's bureaucratic fiefdom is understandable and even predictable—but such impulses cannot be accommodated if they result in a lessening of First Amendment freedoms. Attorneys general are thus adding to the already intense pressure on the First Amendment that has traditionally been applied by Congress and the Federal Trade Commission.

Twenty Years of Trying

One might assume that we singled out 1990 because it was an especially fruitful year for ill-conceived proposals to restrict advertising. Actually it was a fairly typical year as far as Congress was concerned. A look at the past two decades shows that members of Congress have been amazingly persistent in trying to limit First Amendment rights by restricting advertising. During the same period the Federal Trade Commission, which has authority to regulate false and misleading advertising, showed bursts of regulatory zeal that were too much even for Congress to stomach, and that certainly exceeded constitutional bounds.

Congress. In March 1970 Congress passed a law (PL 91-222) that banned all cigarette commercials on radio, television, and other electronic media as of Jan. 2, 1971. (By making the effective date Jan. 2, Congress allowed cigarette companies one last televised shot at the large audiences watching New Year's Day bowl games.) The legislation also required stronger warning labels on cigarette packs, kept regulatory authority for tobacco ads in federal hands, and prohibited the FTC from requiring health warnings in print ads before July 1, 1971. The justification for the radio and TV ad ban was that the government (through the Federal Communications Commission) had the authority to regulate the airwaves in the public interest; smoking was judged inimical to that interest, and thus the government sought to ban such advertising in the electronic venues it controlled.

Perhaps it is not surprising that this ban, the most sweeping restriction in the history of advertising, was enacted at a low point in commercial speech jurisprudence. Between 1942 and 1975 the Supreme Court did not recognize First Amendment rights for commercial speech and therefore the ban did not trigger constitutional concerns in 1970. This was also a low point for the rights of broadcasters—a time when the Court tolerated some fairly heavy-handed regulation. Thus recent history gives us a striking example of what can happen to the First Amendment when well-meaning legislators are not checked by the Supreme Court.

The trend continued in 1973 when Congress passed legislation banning radio and television ads for "little cigars" (cigarette-shaped cigars that had eluded the earlier ban). Legislation introduced in 1982 would have required stronger, rotating warnings and other disclosures on cigarette labels. It went nowhere, but similar proposals were introduced—and left hanging—again in 1983. Finally in 1984, a new version by Rep. Albert Gore, Jr. (D-Tenn.) became law and required one of four rotating Surgeon General's warnings to appear on labels and in ads. Legislation to require warnings in packaging and advertising for snuff and chewing tobacco was introduced in 1985 but languished. In 1986, however, Congress did pass a measure that required warning labels *and* banned radio and television ads for so-called "smokeless" tobacco. This example demonstrates the power of precedent, which prevailed here despite the more protected environment for commercial speech that existed in early 1986.

Attempts to impose labeling requirements on alcohol beverage containers also showed great staying power. A Senate measure in 1986, for example, would have required four rotating warnings on product labels. Finally in 1988 a labeling measure by Sen. Strom Thurmond (R-S.C.) was successfully included in an omnibus anti-drug law (PL 100-690). A testimony to persistence, Sen. Thurmond had been pushing alcohol warning-label legislation without luck every year since 1971.

Children's advertising is another subject with a long congressional history. In 1973, for example, the Senate Select Committee on Nutrition and Human Needs held hearings on television advertising of food to children, with a focus on presweetened breakfast cereals. Among the witnesses was a professor of nutrition from Harvard University who stated apocalyptically that TV advertising of sugary foods was "nothing short of a national disaster" and called for a ban on kids' food ads.

What does the performance of the U.S. Congress over the last two decades teach us? Several lessons come to mind:

- Legislators are nothing if not persistent. Few regulatory schemes were enacted in the year they were proposed. Many were multi-year, multi-session undertakings. Thus, today's legislative fiasco might be law in two, three, or five years.
- Labeling requirements on packages have a way of growing into labeling requirements in advertisements. Labeling requirements in advertisements have a way of growing into advertising bans. One need only study the legislative histories of cigarette, smokeless tobacco, and alcohol restrictions.
- A little precedent goes a long way. The radio and TV ban for cigarettes in 1970 was followed by a similar ban for little cigars in 1973, followed by a smokeless tobacco ad ban in 1986 (a relatively balmy time for commercial speech rights at that). The precedent for ad bans is already established. Where will it lead next?
- Congress is not concerned with the constitutional aspects of advertising restrictions. Congressmen have proved all too willing to sacrifice First Amendment concerns in attempts to regulate unpopular products.
- The First Amendment generally fares better during periods when the Supreme Court keeps Congress in check. This is why the present need is so urgent for the Court to strengthen its position on commercial speech protection.

Federal Trade Commission. From a regulatory perspective, commercial speech has historically come under the purview of the Federal Trade Commission (FTC). Commercial speech that is false or misleading is not entitled to First Amendment protection, and is subject to government action under Section 5 of the Federal Trade Commission Act[8] which states that false and misleading advertising is unlawful. Over the years the FTC has regulated advertising with varying degrees of zeal, prompting debate (and occasional congressional action) concerning its role. In 1969, for example, the FTC proposed tough warning messages for cigarette advertising; when Congress banned radio and TV cigarette ads in 1970, it also barred the FTC from implementing that proposal for print ads until July 1, 1971.

On a broader scale the FTC reached a turning point in 1974. The Magnuson-Moss Act (PL 93-637) gave the FTC sweeping authority to issue industry-wide rules with the force of law, and required due-process hearings and cross-examination rights for affected parties. This gave the FTC power over broad economic interest groups rather than individual businesses, and gave it a quasi-legislative power that many in Congress resented. A five-year congressional budget battle ensued, and Congress did not relent until it gave itself veto power over FTC actions and clarified FTC authority. The Federal Trade Commission Improvement Act of 1980 (PL 96-252) banned the FTC for two years from promulgating regulations based on the concept of "unfair" advertising as opposed to false or deceptive advertising.

In late 1980 the Consumer Subcommittee of the Senate Commerce, Science, and Transportation Committee announced plans to hold hearings on this "unfairness" concept. In a statement to the subcommittee, the FTC acknowledged that the First Amendment places strict limits "upon the extent to which the government may regulate non-deceptive commercial speech, but further believes that the First Amendment does not entirely preclude such regulation." Noting the Supreme Court's decision earlier that year in *Central Hudson*,[9] the FTC said it would "proceed with caution as the courts contrive to refine the standards for governmental regulation of nondeceptive commercial speech."

The Commission issued a policy statement in 1983 that clarified its position on deception:

> The Commission will find an act or practice deceptive if there is a misrepresentation, omission, or other practice, that misleads the consumer acting reasonably in the circumstances, to the consumer's detriment.[10]

In the following year the FTC published its position on advertising substantiation and noted its intent "to continue vigorous enforcement of this existing legal requirement that advertisers substantiate express and implied claims, however conveyed, that make objective assertions about the item or service advertised."[11] The Commission said that "consumers expect a 'reasonable basis' for claims," and listed six factors that would determine whether a reasonable basis existed:

- Type of claim.
- Product.
- Consequences of a false claim.
- Benefits of a truthful claim.
- Cost of developing substantiation for the claim.
- Amount of substantiation experts in the field believe is reasonable.

In an accompanying analysis, the Commission's Bureau of Consumer Protection noted that "consumers might reasonably expect greater substantiation for dietary, medical, safety, and efficacy claims than for more general claims," because such claims may be more specific or detailed than other types.[12]

The current FTC chairman, Janet Steiger, has pledged to make the regulation of national advertising a priority. The Commission has identified a number of topics for scrutiny, including environmental claims (*e.g.*, biodegradability); ads targeted to underage users of alcohol and tobacco; program-length commercials ("infomercials"); medical claims; cosmetics; products advertised to children; and food. (It should be noted that the FTC has primary authority to regulate *advertising* containing health or medical claims. The Food and Drug

Administration (FDA) is responsible for regulating health claims and nutrition information appearing on product *labels*.)

Under current commercial speech doctrine, advertising found by the FTC to be false or misleading would not be entitled to any First Amendment protections. In this regard the Supreme Court's decision in *Peel v. Attorney Registration and Disciplinary Commission of Illinois*[13] is significant: By expressly rejecting the notion that *potentially* misleading ads could be restricted, the Court preserved the regulatory status quo and foreclosed the possibility of imposing regulatory constraints on a far broader range of ads.

•　　•　　•

If this look at current developments and historical trends tells us anything, it is this: Congress, the FTC, state legislatures, and state attorneys general habitually pursue agendas that are hostile to the First Amendment in the realm of commercial speech. Congress has demonstrated a perennial penchant for proposing bad legislation, but recent offerings such as the Gore/Kennedy alcohol ad restrictions and the Kennedy and Waxman tobacco ad restrictions are among the most hurtful to the First Amendment we have ever seen. If history gives any clue, however, some version of these may well become law in the future just by virtue of persistence if not merit. Meanwhile the Federal Trade Commission, possessed of a long history of regulatory excess, may be about to enter another phase of aggressive regulation following a period of atypical moderation. And state attorneys general are acting more aggressively than ever before in creating new opportunities to regulate advertising.

None of this bodes well for the future of commercial speech or the First Amendment. Our only hope for relief is the Supreme Court—but the Court's record on commercial speech has been changeable, and of late has been gravitating toward less protection. Before we begin to explore the reasons for the Court's twists, turns, and apparent contradictions, let us examine some of the pivotal cases in commercial speech jurisprudence.

II. Commercial Speech Jurisprudence:
A Fifty-Year Odyssey

The doctrine of commercial speech (and the legal cottage industry that has grown up around it) was born in a four-page Supreme Court decision in 1942. In *Valentine v. Chrestensen*,[14] the Court ruled that a handbill that contained advertising on one side and a civic protest on the other was subject to a municipal restriction prohibiting the distribution of "commercial and business advertising matter."[15]

Chrestensen was the owner of a former U.S. Navy submarine, which he brought to New York City in 1940 and moored at a state pier in the East River. He planned to sell admission tickets, and toward that end he printed and tried to distribute fliers advertising his attraction. He was advised by the police commissioner, Valentine, that he was violating Section 318 of the Sanitary Code which prohibited such distribution. He then prepared a double-faced handbill—on one side he retained the advertising, and on the other he added a protest against the New York City Dock Department for refusing to provide dockage for his submarine. The police department advised him that a handbill containing only the protest would be acceptable, but he proceeded to distribute the two-sided version and was restrained.

The Court took but two paragraphs to dispose of the matter. "This court has unequivocally held that the streets are proper places for the exercise of freedom of communicating information and disseminating opinion and that . . . states and municipalities . . . may not unduly burden or proscribe its employment in these public thoroughfares. We are equally clear that the Constitution imposes no such restraint on government as respects purely commercial advertising."[16] The Court did not, however, offer any clues as to how it achieved this clarity, since the Constitution says nothing about commercial advertising.

The Court was not moved by the addition of the protest to the handbill, noting that Chrestensen had added it only to evade the prohibition of the ordinance. "If that evasion were successful, every merchant who desires to broadcast advertising leaflets in the streets need only append a civic appeal, or a moral platitude, to achieve immunity from the law's command," the Court said.[17]

In rendering its decision, the Court reversed the U.S. Court of Appeals for the Second Circuit. The lower court had also drawn a distinction between protected speech and advertising, but was persuaded that the protest message served to protect the handbill's advertising content. In noting that the advertising flier also contained information in the public interest, the lower court displayed an awareness of one of the issue's key definitional problems—an awareness that would not be demonstrated by the Supreme Court for three decades.

Referring to *Valentine* in 1959, Justice Douglas said: "The ruling was casual, almost offhand. And it has not survived reflection."[18] In a footnote he implied that *Valentine* was not authoritative in determining the relationship between advertising regulation and the First Amendment.[19]

In *Pittsburgh Press Co. v. Pittsburgh Commission on Human Relations*,[20] the Court upheld as constitutional a city ordinance that prohibited newspapers from running employment ads under gender-specific titles (*e.g.*, Help Wanted—Male). The Court's decision in 1973 again drew the distinction between commercial and other speech, but is most remembered for giving us the classic definition of commercial speech: speech that does "no more than propose a commercial transaction."[21]

Two years later the Court seemed to agree with Justice Douglas that *Valentine* had not survived reflection. In *Bigelow v. Virginia*[22] the Court said that the fact that a particular advertisement "had commercial aspects or reflected the advertiser's commercial interests did not negate all First Amendment guarantees."[23]

Bigelow was the managing editor of the *Virginia Weekly*, a newspaper circulated in Albemarle County, Virginia (which includes Charlottesville and the University of Virginia). On Feb. 8, 1971, his paper ran an ad for the Women's Pavilion, an abortion-referral service in New York City. Under the headline "Unwanted Pregnancy—Let Us Help You," the ad said, among other things: "Abortions are now legal in New York. There are no residency requirements. For immediate placements in accredited hospitals and clinics at low cost contact Women's Pavilion. . . . Strictly confidential. We will make all arrangements for you and help you with information and counseling."[24] Trouble was, abortions were then illegal in Virginia, and a statute dating from 1878 made it a misdemeanor to encourage the procurement of abortions in Virginia through advertising or other means.

In upholding lower-court convictions, the Virginia Supreme Court asserted the state's interest in promoting quality medical care for its residents. But the U.S. Supreme Court dismissed that interest, saying that: "A State does not acquire power or supervision over the internal affairs of another State merely because the welfare and health of its own citizens may be affected when they travel to that State."[25] The Court said that Virginia "may not, under the guise of exercising internal police powers, bar a citizen of another State from disseminating information about an activity that is legal in that State."[26]

In addition, the Court noted that Virginia had erred in assuming "that advertising, as such, was entitled to no First Amendment protection,"[27] and had thereby overlooked Bigelow's First Amendment rights. In the end, the Court said, Virginia had failed to balance Bigelow's rights against its asserted interest in the welfare of its citizens, an interest that was tantamount to regulating what Virginia residents may hear or read about New York services.

An important element in *Bigelow* was the claim that the ad contained informational elements and thus did more than propose a commercial transaction. The Court cited the lines "Abortions are now legal in New York. There are no residency requirements" as an example of non-commercial information the ad conveyed. Since the Court had earlier ruled that ordinary speech appearing in the form of a paid advertisement does not lose its protection,[28] the presence of these informational elements amid the ad's solicitation entitled the ad to a higher level of protection.

Bigelow is significant because it marks the coming together, if not the complete crystallization, of many of the elements that were to become building blocks of the Court's commercial speech doctrine. Foremost, it reaffirmed (contrary to *Valentine*) that commercial speech is entitled to some degree of protection—presumably in proportion to the extent that the speech does more than propose a commercial transaction. It stressed that protection does not extend to the advertising of illegal activities; it stopped short of deciding the precise extent of allowable regulation of advertising for activities the state can regulate or ban. It emphasized the need to balance First Amendment protection against the interests of the government, and restated a standard of "reasonable regulation that serves a legitimate public interest." And it said *Valentine* should be regarded merely as a restriction on the manner of distribution, and not as a "sweeping proposition that advertising should be unprotected *per se*." By the time the Court was finished with *Bigelow* it had restored to commercial speech some of what *Valentine* had taken away.[29]

Eleven months later the Court revisited the issue and continued, through a shift in philosophic gears, to strengthen protections for commercial speech. *Virginia State Board of Pharmacy v. Virginia Citizens Consumer Council, Inc.*[30] addressed a Virginia statute that prohibited licensed pharmacists from advertising the price of prescription drugs. The appellees, as consumers of prescription drugs, had challenged the ad ban; their position was upheld by a three-judge District Court.

Here was a case that dealt solely with the paradigm example of commercial speech, price advertising—speech that does "no more than propose a commercial transaction." The case was not complicated by the legality of the underlying activity as in *Pittsburgh Press*, or by statements of fact or opinion of a general public interest contained in the ad as in *Bigelow*. As the Court succinctly put it:

> [T]he question whether there is a First Amendment exception for "commercial speech" is squarely before us. Our pharmacist does not wish to editorialize on any subject, cultural, philosophical, or political. He does not wish to report any particularly newsworthy fact, or to make generalized observations even about commercial matters. The "idea" he wishes to communicate is simply this: "I will sell you the X prescription drug at the Y price." Our question, then, is whether this communication is wholly outside the protection of the First Amendment.[31]

No, the Court went on to answer itself, the communication is not without protection. Although the speaker's interest may be purely economic, that hardly disqualifies him from protection under the First Amendment. The Court cited an analogous example of labor disputes, where the interests of management and labor are primarily economic but the speech of both sides is protected nonetheless.

The Court broke some new ground when it addressed the interest of the consumer in receiving price information:

> If there is a right to advertise, there is a reciprocal right to receive the advertising, and it may be asserted by these appellees.[32]

In so stating, the Court was extending to commercial speech First Amendment doctrine granting constitutional rights to the recipients of messages. "Freedom of speech presupposes a willing speaker. But where a speaker exists, as is the case here, the protection afforded is to the communication, to its source and to its recipients both."[33] The Court cited *Lamont v. Postmaster General*[34] (First Amendment rights of citizens to receive political publications from abroad);

Kleindienst v. Mandel[35] (First Amendment right to "receive information and ideas," and that freedom of speech "'necessarily protects the right to receive'"); and *Procunier v. Martinez*[36] (censorship of prisoners' mail infringes First Amendment rights of recipients).

In a statement that is anathema to purists in the political-speech camp, the Court assessed the importance of economic information to the contemporary citizen/consumer:

> As to the particular consumer's interest in the free flow of commercial information, that interest may be as keen, if not keener by far, than his interest in the day's most urgent political debate.[37]

The other remarkable aspect of this decision is that the Court rejected the balancing-of-values approach in *Bigelow* and previous cases, opting instead for a principled constitutional rationale for protecting commercial speech. Virginia had asserted an interest in banning pharmacist price advertising to protect its citizens. It feared that the advertising of prices would lure consumers into choosing low-cost, low-quality service, destroy the pharmacist-customer relationship, and cause consumers to lose respect for the pharmacy profession.

The Court rejected this approach, calling it "highly paternalistic," and suggested an alternative:

> That alternative is to assume that this information is not in itself harmful, that people will perceive their own best interests if only they are well enough informed, and that the best means to that end is to open the channels of communication rather than to close them. . . . But the choice among these alternative approaches is not ours to make or the Virginia General Assembly's. It is precisely this kind of choice, between the dangers of suppressing information, and the dangers of its misuse if it is freely available, that the First Amendment makes for us.[38]

Virginia Pharmacy Board was, and still is, the Supreme Court's high-water mark in its consideration of commercial speech. Its emphasis on the rights of listeners to receive information has pivotal implications in developing a new framework for protecting commercial speech, as we shall attempt to do in later chapters. And its emphasis on the primacy of the First Amendment over asserted state interests (and concomitant rejection of values balancing) was a refreshing triumph of principle over relativism—a triumph that unfortunately would prove to be short lived.

The pieces of commercial speech doctrine that had been emerging during the 1970s were finally patched together in a four-part test enunciated in *Central Hudson Gas & Electric Corp. v. Public Service Commission of New York*,[39] decided in June 1980. But the Court's patchwork quilt bore a stronger resemblance to *Bigelow*, with its emphasis on the balancing of competing values, than to *Virginia Pharmacy Board's* reliance on the primacy of the First Amendment.[40]

Central Hudson was challenging a 1973 regulation of the Public Service Commission of New York which banned all promotional advertising by an electric utility. The ban was enacted to help reduce electric consumption at a time when the Commission believed the state's utility system could not meet additional demand. Central Hudson opposed the ban on First Amendment grounds when the Commission reviewed the regulation three years later, but the policy was extended.

In continuing the prohibition, the Commission distinguished two categories of advertising: promotional, and institutional and informational. Promotional advertising, which sought to stimulate the purchase of utility services, was deemed by the Commission to be contrary to national energy-conservation goals and thus was banned. However, the Commission explicitly allowed institutional and informational advertising, a broadly defined category with the general goal of shifting consumption during peak times to off-peak times, thereby reducing the need for additional generating capacity. Central Hudson mounted a judicial challenge to the ban, again on First Amendment grounds, but the Commission's position was upheld by the state trial court and appellate courts. The New York Court of Appeals concluded that the government's interests outweighed the advertising's limited constitutional value.[41]

The Court used *Central Hudson* as an opportunity to restate and consolidate many of its previous thoughts on commercial speech. It cited *Virginia Pharmacy Board's* rejection of the paternalistic notion that government has complete power to regulate commercial speech and that the First Amendment protects commercial speech from unwarranted regulation.[42] The Court restated that the First Amendment's concern for commercial speech is in its "information function,"[43] and that the government may therefore ban commercial speech that is "more likely to deceive the public than to inform it."[44] The Court also noted that First Amendment remedies must be narrowly drawn.

Justice Powell's opinion for the Court summed up the resulting test:

> In commercial speech cases, then, a four-part analysis has developed. At the outset, we must determine whether the expression is protected by the First Amendment. For commercial speech to come within that provision, it at least must concern lawful activity and not be misleading. Next, we ask whether the asserted governmental interest is substantial. If both inquiries yield positive answers, we must determine whether the regulation directly advances the governmental interest asserted, and whether it is not more extensive than is necessary to serve that interest.[45]

Applying this test to the facts in *Central Hudson*, the Court recognized that the activity was legal and that the Commission was not claiming the speech to be misleading. Having cleared this threshold, the Court considered the state's interest and concluded that the Commission order directly advanced the state's interest in energy conservation.[46] The Court struck down the regulation on the grounds that the advertising ban was more extensive than necessary to serve the state's interest. "In the absence of a showing that more limited speech regulation would be ineffective, we cannot approve the complete suppression of Central Hudson's advertising," the Court concluded.[47]

Commercial speech doctrine took an odd twist in 1986 in a narrow 5-4 decision. *Posadas de Puerto Rico Associates v. Tourism Company of Puerto Rico*[48] embellished governmental regulatory authority by stating that the government's power to ban an activity also includes the power to ban the advertising of that activity.

Under Puerto Rico's Games of Chance Act of 1948, casino gambling is permitted to promote tourism, but there is a catch: " '[n]o gambling room shall be permitted to advertise or otherwise offer their facilities to the public of Puerto Rico.' "[49] Puerto Ricans are allowed to gamble in the casinos, but may not be enticed there by advertising. Posadas de Puerto Rico Associates, a partnership that operated the Condado Holiday Inn Hotel and Sands Casino, was fined by the Tourism Company of Puerto Rico (a public corporation that administers the Act) for violating the Act and its implementing regulations regarding the local ad ban.

Posadas sued, claiming that its commercial speech had been suppressed in violation of the First Amendment; it also sought relief under the equal protection and due process clauses of the Constitution. The Puerto Rico Superior Court held that the ad ban had been applied unconstitutionally to Posadas' past conduct, but then narrowed the construction of the Act and regulations so as to restrict advertising aimed specifically at residents but to allow local advertising aimed at tourists that might also be seen by residents. Based on this construction, the court said, the Act and regulations were facially unconstitutional. The Puerto Rico Supreme Court dismissed Posadas' appeal, saying that a "substantial constitutional question" was not presented.[50]

The U.S. Supreme Court regarded the matter as one of "pure commercial speech which does 'no more than propose a commercial transaction,' "[51] and thus applied the four-part *Central Hudson* test. First the Court acknowledged that the issue involved a legal activity (casino gambling) and that the advertising was not misleading or fraudulent. Next the Court addressed the government's interest in regulating the speech at issue, a desire to reduce casino gambling by Puerto Rican residents. According to the Tourism Company's brief, the Puerto Rican legislature believed that " '[e]xcessive casino gambling among local residents. . .would produce serious harmful effects on the health, safety, and welfare of the Puerto Rican citizens, such as the disruption of moral and cultural patterns, the increase in local crime, the fostering of prostitution, the development of corruption, and the infiltration of organized crime.' "[52] The Court had "no difficulty" determining that this was a " 'substantial' governmental interest."[53] Moving to *Central Hudson's* third test, the Court concluded that the restriction on advertising to residents did directly advance the government's interest. On the fourth test, "whether the restrictions on commercial speech are no more extensive than necessary to serve the government's interest," the Court said they were not. "The narrowing constructions of the advertising restrictions announced by the Superior Court ensure that the restrictions will not affect advertising of casino gambling aimed at tourists, but will apply only to such advertising when aimed at the residents of Puerto Rico."[54] The Court concluded, based on its application of the *Central Hudson* test, that the Puerto Rico Supreme Court was correct in rejecting Posadas' First Amendment claim.

The Court then articulated what amounted to a new principle of commercial speech doctrine:

> In our view, the greater power to completely ban casino gambling necessarily includes the lesser power to ban advertising of casino gambling. . . . [I]t is precisely *because* the government could have enacted a wholesale prohibition of the underlying conduct that it is permissible for the government to take the less intrusive step of allowing the conduct, but reducing the demand through restrictions on advertising.[55]

As regulatory precedent among state legislatures, the Court cited a 1986 Nevada statute authorizing the licensing of houses of prostitution in sparsely populated counties, but prohibiting the advertising of such establishments.

Posadas hardly represented a judicial consensus. Justice Brennan, joined by Justices Marshall and Blackmun, dissented sharply and said the last three prongs of the *Central Hudson* test had not been met. Justice Stevens, again with Justices Marshall and Blackmun, offered a separate dissent.

The impact of *Posadas* has been the subject of considerable discussion. On the one hand it extended the government's regulatory grasp to advertising for products or services which themselves could be banned (a bad omen, perhaps, for liquor and cigarettes), but on the other it did preserve the four-part analysis of *Central Hudson*. *Posadas'* effect on the future of commercial speech may be muted somewhat by the case's unusual facts, the Court's apparent deference to the Puerto Rican social and cultural climate, and the spirited dissent within the Court. Overall, though, *Posadas* was hardly a victory for commercial speech rights.

First Amendment rights for commercial speech were eroded significantly and incontrovertibly in a 1989 opinion written by Justice Scalia. In *Board of Trustees of the State University of New York v. Fox*,[56] the Court weakened *Central Hudson's* fourth test that calls for regulation of protected commercial speech to be the "least restrictive means" available, and substituted a criterion of "reasonable means."

In 1982 a salesperson for American Future Systems, Inc. (AFS) conducted a party-style demonstration of the company's housewares for a group of students in a dormitory room on S.U.N.Y.'s Cortland campus. She was arrested by campus police for violating a S.U.N.Y. regulation that states: "No authorization will be given to private commercial enterprises to operate on State University campuses or in facilities furnished by the University. . . ."[57] Fox and other students, joined by AFS, sued for declaratory judgment in District Court alleging that the prohibition of the sales presentation violated their First Amendment rights. After granting a preliminary injunction, the District Court later ruled at trial in favor of the university, concluding that S.U.N.Y. dormitories did not constitute a public forum and that the speech restrictions were permissible given the dormitories' function. That decision was reversed and remanded by the Second Circuit Court of Appeals,[58] which directed the trial court to determine whether the S.U.N.Y. regulation "directly advanced the State's asserted interests and whether, if it did, it was the least restrictive means to that end."[59]

The Court, falling back on the *Pittsburgh Press* definition of commercial speech (to "propose a commercial transaction"), concluded that the sales party was indeed commercial speech. The appellants argued that the party also included elements of noncommercial (*i.e.*, fully protected) speech, such as information on home economics. Without mentioning *Valentine v. Chrestensen*, Justice Scalia hearkened back to Chrestensen's two-sided handbills in dismissing that claim: "Including these home economics elements no more converted AFS's presentations into educational speech, than opening sales presentations with a prayer or a Pledge of Allegiance would convert them into religious or political speech."[60] The Court announced its intention to review the case in light of *Central Hudson's* four-part test, and launched into a lengthy discussion of its interpretations of "least restrictive means" in a host of previous cases:

> Our cases have repeatedly stated that government restrictions upon commercial speech may be no more broad or no more expansive than "necessary" to serve its substantial interests. . . . We have indeed assumed in dicta the validity of the "least restrictive means" approach. . . . And other formulations in our commercial speech cases support a more flexible meaning for the *Central Hudson* test. . . . Whatever the conflicting tenor of our prior dicta may be, we now focus upon this specific issue for the first time, and conclude that the reason of the matter requires something short of a least-restrictive-means standard.[61]

The Court went on to elaborate what it had in mind:

> What our decisions require is a " 'fit' between the legislature's ends and the means chosen to accomplish those ends,". . .—a fit that is not necessarily perfect, but reasonable; that represents not necessarily the single best disposition but one whose scope is "in proportion to the interest served,". . .that employs not necessarily the least restrictive means but, as we have put it in other contexts discussed above, a means narrowly tailored to achieve the desired objective.[62]

With a burst of judicial restraint, the Court concluded that "[w]ithin those bounds we leave it to governmental decisionmakers to judge what manner of regulation may best be employed."[63] The Court went on to address an overbreadth challenge, but determined that it was not ripe for resolution. It then remanded the case to the trial court to determine, based on the new standards, "the validity of this law's application to the commercial and noncommercial speech that is the subject of the complaint" and, if so, to determine if "its substantial overbreadth nonetheless makes it unenforceable."[64] The case was not settled, but new damage had been done to commercial speech's constitutional protection.

Attorney Advertising

The Republic was not long into its third century when members of the bar threw in their lot with purveyors of drugs, real estate, and prophylactics[65] and began asserting a First Amendment right to advertise. Attorney advertising quickly became a sidebar to the feature story of commercial speech, or, as one pair of commentators put it, "the doctrinal trunk sprouted an entirely new branch."[66] This section will review briefly the judicial history of commercial speech as applied to attorney advertising, especially as certain of these cases have spawned doctrinal interpretations or definitions that have been applied to general commercial speech cases.

In 1977, one year after *Virginia Pharmacy Board* (and three years before *Central Hudson* and its four-part test), the Supreme Court addressed the question of whether attorneys may engage in price advertising for routine legal services. In *Bates v. State Bar of Arizona*[67] the Court ruled that advertising for Bates' legal clinic was not misleading and fell under the scope of First Amendment protection. The Court cited a number of potential benefits in attorney advertising, such as reducing consumers' legal costs, aiding new attorneys in entering the market, and benefiting the administration of justice. In reaching its decision the Court appeared to weigh the benefits against potential drawbacks such as misleading consumers, driving up legal costs, and diminishing the status of the legal profession. Although the decision came only a year after the Court had affirmed the primacy of the First Amendment in *Virginia Pharmacy Board*, the Court's 5-4 ruling in *Bates* retreated to the balancing-of-values approach taken earlier in *Bigelow*:

> [W]e are not persuaded that any of the proffered justifications rise to the level of an acceptable reason for the suppression of all advertising by attorneys.[68]

In re Primus,[69] decided in 1978, concerned an attorney for the American Civil Liberties Union (ACLU) who had written to a woman to inform her that the ACLU was interested in filing a lawsuit against a physician on her behalf. The Court said this was not a commercial speech case and decided on the grounds of the attorney's right of free association. However, the Court did say that time, place, and manner restrictions could be placed on solicitation, and that the government could ban "in-person solicitation for pecuniary gain."

Ohralik v. Ohio State Bar Association,[70] also decided in 1978, involved an attorney who visited an automobile accident victim in the hospital and convinced her to become his client. This in-person solicitation brought him an indefinite suspension from the Supreme Court of Ohio, which the Court upheld. Noting commercial speech's "subordinate position in the scale of First Amendment values," the Court again used a balancing approach to conclude that Ohralik's behavior was "subject to regulation in furtherance of important state interests."

In re R.M.J.[71] was the first post-*Central Hudson* case to address professional advertising. The attorney in this instance was reprimanded by the Supreme Court of Missouri for failing to follow prescribed language in advertising the types of legal services he offered. Also at issue was his mailing of announcement cards to a broader group than that allowed under rules for professional advertising promulgated by an Advisory Committee of the Missouri Supreme Court.

In 1982 the U.S. Supreme Court reversed the state court's judgment in a unanimous opinion, relying on the tests in *Central Hudson*. The Court found that the ads in question were not misleading (as distinguished from merely being in bad taste), and that the Advisory

Committee's rules were more restrictive than necessary in advancing the state's interests. "Although the potential for deception and confusion is particularly strong in the context of advertising professional services, restrictions upon such advertising may be no broader than reasonably necessary to prevent the deception," the Court said.[72] Justice Powell's opinion for the Court summarized the Court's position on commercial speech doctrine in the context of advertising for professional services:

> Truthful advertising related to lawful activities is entitled to the protections of the First Amendment. But when the particular content or method of the advertising suggests that it is inherently misleading or when experience has proved that in fact such advertising is subject to abuse, the States may impose appropriate restrictions. Misleading advertising may be prohibited entirely.[73]

The Court went on to reiterate the principles of the *Central Hudson* test, thereby muting the protection it seemed to be extending in the opening sentence above.

Zauderer v. Office of Disciplinary Counsel[74] concerned an attorney who advertised his availability to represent women who wished to pursue claims against the maker of the Dalkon Shield contraceptive device. In reversing an Ohio Supreme Court disciplinary action, the Court again relied on the *Central Hudson* analysis in determining that the state did not have a sufficient interest in restricting such ads. However, the Court did uphold a state disclosure requirement regarding contingent fees and court costs although it acknowledged the potential First Amendment impact of mandatory speech. In imposing this further restriction on commercial speech the Court sounded an ominous note for advertisers of consumer goods: "We hold that an advertiser's rights are adequately protected as long as disclosure requirements are reasonably related to the State's interest in preventing deception of consumers."[75]

Shapero v. Kentucky Bar Association[76] involved an attorney who sent solicitation letters to individuals facing foreclosure suits, in violation of a state regulation prohibiting such targeted mailings. The

Court ruled in favor of the attorney, distinguishing his direct-mail solicitation from in-person solicitation, and finding the ban on such letters overly broad as measured by *Central Hudson*.

In dissent, however, Justice O'Connor (joined by Chief Justice Rehnquist and Justice Scalia) spoke in language that seemed to limit still further the type of commercial speech that should receive some protection:

> States should have considerable latitude to ban advertising that is "potentially or demonstrably misleading". . .as well as truthful advertising that undermines the substantial governmental interest in promoting the high ethical standards that are necessary in the legal profession.[77]

To suggest that states be able to ban "potentially misleading" advertising is to suggest that states be given authority to ban *all* advertising, since any ad can be construed to be *potentially* misleading in some aspect to someone—a potential event is only a possibility, by definition something not proved in fact. Moreover, the further suggestion that a ban be extended to truthful advertising far exceeds *Central Hudson's* test that a remedy be the "least restrictive means" available.

Shortly after the 1989 *S.U.N.Y.* decision weakened commercial speech protection by substituting "reasonable means" for "least restrictive means," commercial speech aficionados mulled the likely fate of Gary Peel. In *Peel v. Attorney Registration and Disciplinary Commission of Illinois*,[78] however, the Court departed from *Central Hudson's* four-part test and took a somewhat broader view of commercial speech based on its importance in making economic decisions. Peel had been censured by the Illinois Supreme Court for including the words "Certified Civil Trial Specialist by the National Board of Trial Advocacy" on his letterhead. In reversing the censure and remanding the case, the Court concluded that the wording was not actually or inherently misleading, although Justice Marshall (joined by Justice Brennan) noted in a separate concurrence that it could be potentially misleading and thus a candidate for additional disclosure language. Generally the outcome was well received by advocates of commercial speech protection, but not because *Peel* did anything to restore the vigor of *Central Hudson's* four-part test.

We can only wonder where the Court will wander next on its commercial speech odyssey.[79] Perhaps the route would be more predictable if we knew that the Court was being guided by a theoretical compass that always pointed toward absolute freedom of speech. But alas, the Court seems to possess no such compass, no such theory. How this has come to be is the subject of the next chapter.

III. Commercial Speech and First Amendment Theory

Commercial speech is a doctrine in search of a theory. From the time it showed up on the doorstep in 1942 (and carrying quite a lot of baggage at that), commercial speech has been the poor relation of the First Amendment family. Some accommodations have been made, often awkwardly, but rare indeed have been the times it has received a warm embrace.

In the 50 years that commercial speech has been recognized as a distinct form of expression, it has been riding a roller coaster of jurisprudence that has taken it from no First Amendment protection (*Valentine*) to significant heights (*Virginia Pharmacy Board* and *Central Hudson*) and back down a series of lesser hills and valleys. Where the ride will end is not known, nor can it be easily predicted. It may seem odd to the casual observer that the Supreme Court has taken so many different positions on the issue—almost, it would seem, to the point of capriciousness. The problem is not that the Court has acted without reason in each instance; rather, the Court has taken reasoned positions but they have been based, at various times, on different interpretations of First Amendment theory, the proper role of the judiciary, and, to a lesser extent, on the definition of commercial speech. What has been lacking is a persuasive constitutional argument, consistently applied, for affording commercial speech full First Amendment protection. This chapter begins by examining the theoretical underpinnings of arguments for and against protection for commercial speech as the first step in what is hoped to be the formulation of a new commercial speech model.

The Constitution

The logical place to begin an examination of commercial speech doctrine is, of course, the Constitution and its First Amendment which reads, in part: "Congress shall make no law. . .abridging the freedom of speech, or of the press." Unfortunately this tells us little about the Founders' views on speech, and nothing about their views on commercial speech, if indeed such a distinction had even crossed their minds.

We must therefore look to the Founders' intentions to try and ascertain if their views on speech are somehow implied in the amendment's wording. The question is this: Did the Founders intend to extend protection to all types of speech (including what we know as commercial speech) since the First Amendment makes no distinction? Yes and no are the answers at which different commentators have arrived.

The "yes" argument suggests that the Founders were men who also had to be concerned with making a living and that this activity was essential to their pursuit of happiness. Commerce, and by extension the advertising of goods for sale, was thus a part of their daily life. Craig R. Smith notes that America's first newspaper, the *Boston News-Letter*, was full of advertising, and that the first version of the Declaration of Independence, printed in the *Pennsylvania Evening Post* on July 6, 1774, shared the page with a full slate of ads.[80] Advertising, already ubiquitous in colonial times, was taken for granted by the Founders as a form of protected speech, the argument goes.

The opposite interpretation suggests that the Founders intended to protect only political speech, because they viewed such speech as vital to the functioning of a self-governing democracy. At the time the Bill of Rights was adopted, James Madison argued that freedom of speech was necessary if citizens were to criticize government officials without fear of reprisal. During the debate over the Alien and Sedition Acts, he emphasized the role of free speech and a free press in giving citizens information about political candidates.[81] As Judge Alex Kozinski and Stuart Banner conclude: "One searches in vain for an indication from any of the people involved with the drafting or ratifying of the first amendment that they were concerned with anything besides politically oriented speech."[82]

But perhaps our question as we have framed it gives the Founders too much credit. Judge Robert Bork has suggested a more dispiriting hypothesis: "The framers seem to have had no coherent theory of free speech and appear not to have been overly concerned with the subject."[83] He suggests that their commitment to free speech was dubious:

> Our forefathers were men accustomed to drawing a line, to us often invisible, between freedom and licentiousness. In colonial times and during and after the Revolution they displayed a determination to punish speech thought dangerous to government, much of it expression that we would think harmless and well within the bounds of legitimate discourse. . . . When Jefferson came to power it developed that he read the first amendment only to limit Congress and he believed suppression to be a proper function of state governments. He appears to have instigated state prosecutions against Federalists for seditious libel. But these later developments do not tell us what the men who adopted the first amendment intended, and their discussions tell us very little either.[84]

As Judge Bork gloomily concludes: "The First Amendment, like the rest of the Bill of Rights, appears to have been a hastily drafted document upon which little thought was expended."[85]

Our first line of inquiry, then, draws a blank; the First Amendment tells us little. Perhaps the Founders intended to protect commercial speech, or perhaps they didn't—or maybe they never thought much

about it. This being the case, perhaps we should next explore the nature
of speech in general and commercial speech in particular. Such an
inquiry, if successful, should shed some light on why commercial
speech has received the treatment it has, and may begin to suggest
some new ways of looking at this type of speech.

The Nature and Function of Speech

Before we ask why we should protect commercial speech, let us
ask why we should protect any type of speech. What is the nature
of speech, what is its unique essence, that moves the Constitution
to elevate it to the stature of a human right? Four arguments are traditionally advanced in explanation of freedom of speech.[86] The first
embraces the idea that speech is central to the concept of human dignity. Speech is something uniquely human, the argument goes, and
is an instrument for self-expression and self-realization. Humans possess an innate dignity that is manifested through the ability to express
oneself through speech. This dignitary function has its locus in the
speaker, not in the listener; in the individual, not in society. An element of toleration is also involved here—speech is tolerated because
it is a reflection of human dignity, not because it is informed or clever
or even important in its own right.

The second argument for free speech is a utilitarian one: the marketplace theory, which holds that truth (or "political truth," if you
will)[87] will be discerned most efficiently if ideas are allowed to com-
pete freely in a "marketplace" where the force of truthful ideas will
drive out untruthful ones. As Justice Brandeis said in his memorable
concurring opinion in *Whitney v. California*:

> Those who won our independence believed that . . . freedom
> to think as you will and to speak as you think are means
> indispensable to the spread and discovery of political truth;
> that without free speech and assembly discussion would be
> futile; that with them, discussion affords ordinarily adequate
> protection against the dissemination of noxious doctrine; that
> the path of safety lies in the opportunity to discuss freely

supposed grievances and proposed remedies; and that the
fitting remedy for evil counsels is good ones.[88]

The utility here is to society, which is presumed to function at a higher
and more efficient level in the presence of the truth.

The third argument for free speech is also utilitarian. It holds that
freedom of speech is necessary to provide the information that
individuals need to make efficient choices in those social mechanisms, such as democracy and capitalism, that function through choice.
"While the 'marketplace of ideas' notion guarantees truth, the choice
notion guarantees the efficient and appropriate operation of both our
political and economic systems."[89] The emphasis here is on the listener
who uses freely available information to make informed political and
economic choices.

Burt Neuborne cites a further argument that has more to do with
freedom of the press—that there is a special "suspicion" about
government:

> This view argues that government cannot be trusted to con-
> trol the flow of information because it is uniquely likely to
> be intolerant, and that the history of power in the world is
> such that one does not trust people with the power to sup-
> press other people's speech because of the unique tendency
> toward intolerance and suppression that is an unfortunate
> aspect of almost any governmental structure.[90]

Of these arguments, we quickly see that three of the four are concerned with protecting speech for its value to the political process.
The other is concerned with speech's expressive, dignitary value, but
even this can include expressions of political opinion. Clearly, then,
political speech possesses a special nature that makes it deserving
of constitutional protection. Of all types of speech, political speech
alone possesses such a strong "dual nature"—its utilitarian value to
the governing process *and* its dignitary value through individual expression of political opinion.

First Amendment court decisions have evolved along these lines,
affording strong protection to political speech and to a broad range

of expressive speech, from door-to-door proselytizing to nude danc-ing.[91] The degree of protection extended to expressive speech has raised the eyebrows of some (like Judge Bork, who would limit protection to speech that is "explicitly political"), but protecting expressive speech—generally covering religion, politics, and the arts—can be rationalized under the human dignity argument outlined above.

Thus, in the areas of religion, politics, and the arts, First Amend-ment theory has been based on two enduring principles: the digni-tary value of self-expression, and the utilitarian value of speech to the political process. Cases falling in these areas can (at least in the-ory) be decided consistently and without too much controversy. The theory works pretty well in these traditional First Amendment areas— but where does commercial speech fit in?

Commercial Speech and Traditional Theory: A Bad Fit

Commercial speech has a problem: It doesn't fit nicely under either principle (dignitary expression or political utilitarianism) of tradi-tional First Amendment theory. Despite occasional attempts to cloak it in political garb, commercial speech is not political speech, which, according to one definition, can be thought of as "criticisms of pub-lic officials and policies, proposals for the adoption or repeal of leg-islation or constitutional provisions and speech addressed to the conduct of any governmental unit in the country."[92]

The reason commercial speech fails as dignitary expression is more interesting, and has to do with the nature of the commercial speaker. The argument is this: Dignitary speech, by definition, has value because it both reflects and promotes the human dignity of its speaker. Because it is a form of *self*-expression, dignitary speech can only be uttered by an individual. But since commercial speech is uttered (for the purpose of this argument) by corporations, it cannot be a form of individual dignitary expression. (We can distinguish this argument from the Supreme Court's ruling in *First National Bank of Boston v. Bellotti*[93] which held that a corporation was capable of uttering pro-tected *political* speech—*i.e.*, utilitarian speech in our model.)

COMMERCIAL SPEECH AND FIRST AMENDMENT THEORY   41

C. Edwin Baker casts the situation in terms of the corporation's structure as a profit-maximizing enterprise; the profit motive becomes paramount in the organization's commercial speech, overshadowing any individual choices or value preferences on the part of the corporation's employees. "The domination of profit, a structurally required standard, breaks the connection between speech and any vision, or attitude, or value of the individual or group engaged in advocacy. Thus, the content and form of commercial speech cannot be attributed to individual value allegiances."[94] Baker's argument is premised on the belief that the First Amendment primarily protects the individual's freedom of choice, or self-expression.

Neuborne is not as rigid in drawing the corporation/individual distinction, but makes a similar point: "You have a [commercial] speaker addressing an issue that is important to him, but it is not the same thing as the conscientiously based notions of self-expression that we had in mind when we thought about religion, political or artistic expression."[95]

This brief overview begins to suggest the dimensions of the problem, at least insofar as First Amendment theory is concerned (there is also a definitional problem, but we shall take that up in the next chapter). The fact that commercial speech does not fall under either political utilitarianism or dignitary expression, the traditional principles of First Amendment theory, suggests three hypotheses:

- The principles are correct and commercial speech properly falls outside the realm of First Amendment protection; *or*
- Current First Amendment theory is inadequate in explaining why commercial speech should receive full First Amendment protection; *or*
- No theory can take into account every circumstance, so we should abandon the search for a general theory and approach the issue on a case-by-case basis, weighing First Amendment values against other values presented in each instance.

Let us hasten to note that we believe the second hypothesis to be the correct one, for reasons we shall develop in Chapter 5. But that opinion is not universally shared. What one commentator calls "the spectacular adventures of the Supreme Court in the now legendary line of [commercial speech] cases"[96] have yielded decisions that have been widely unpredictable precisely because the Court has preferred to vacillate between hypotheses one and three (with a brief detour—*Virginia Pharmacy Board*—in the direction of two). And of course hypothesis three in itself offers, and in fact practically guarantees, endless possibilities for inconsistency. It would be helpful to pause here and consider hypothesis three since the benchmark of contemporary commercial speech jurisprudence, the four-part test of *Central Hudson* as modified in *S.U.N.Y.*, is essentially an attempt to balance First Amendment values against other values.

The Rationale for Balancing Values

There is a strong and persistent strain of thought in First Amendment analysis that makes a case for balancing free speech values against other values. This thinking argues that it is pointless to try and develop an all-encompassing theory about freedom of speech; rather, it is considered more productive to employ a case-by-case approach. This necessarily implies a balancing of First Amendment versus other values, and is based on the assumption that the First Amendment right to free speech is not an absolute. Writing in the year before *Central Hudson* was decided, Daniel A. Farber addressed the difficulty of developing a suitable theory:

> The problems raised by the regulation of entirely truthful speech do not lend themselves to unified analysis. The topic itself is too amorphous for comprehensive treatment. All that connects the cases is the fact that the claimed justification for regulation is something other than the prevention of deception. Obviously, a state could claim any number of possible justifications, each potentially requiring separate treatment. . . . The best approach to the topic is probably to discuss the problems on a case-by-case basis, just as the Court is forced to confront them.[97]

In an article written during the *Central Hudson* era (1983), Steven Shiffrin also favored the balancing approach:

> [T]he courts have not always been wrong in permitting the state to outlaw the dissemination of truth. Speech is important, but so are the values of privacy, security, and reputation. Although we might question many of the specific accommodations in this area, the problems lie in particular contexts; the process of making accommodations is appropriate.[98]

Toward the end of the Dark Age of commercial speech regulation (1942-1975), Judge Bork (while still a professor at Yale Law School) addressed the absolutist question in his 1971 article on neutral principles:

> In framing a theory of free speech the first obstacle is the insistence of many very intelligent people that the "first amendment is an absolute.". . .Any such reading is, of course, impossible. Since it purports to be an absolute position we are entitled to test it with extreme hypotheticals. Is Congress forbidden to prohibit incitement to mutiny aboard a naval vessel engaged in action against an enemy, to prohibit shouted harangues from the visitors' gallery during its own deliberations or to provide any rules for decorum in federal courtrooms?. . .No one, not the most obsessed absolutist, takes any such position, but if one does not, the absolute position is abandoned, revealed as a play on words.[99]

There can be no argument with Judge Bork that freedom of speech is, in practice, less than absolute. We do not countenance harmful speech of an expressive nature (such as falsely yelling "fire" in a crowded theater), nor do we countenance harmful speech that might have some utilitarian value for the listener (such as publishing information on troop and ship movements during wartime).

But examples like these could lead us to overlook an important distinction. We should distinguish between treating freedom of speech as merely one more value to be balanced against equal, competing values, as opposed to the concept of First Amendment primacy— that freedom of speech holds a special constitutionally protected place in our society, and that it should be subjected to balancing against lesser (though important) values only in the extreme.

In *United States v. O'Brien*,[100] a case in which an anti-war protester petitioned unsuccessfully that the act of burning his draft card in public was a form of protected free speech, the Court adopted a balancing test that recognized the primacy of the First Amendment. In determining whether a government regulation is justified, the Court established a four-part test that the regulation must meet:

- The regulation must be within the constitutional power of the government.
- It must further an important or substantial governmental interest.
- The governmental interest must be unrelated to the suppression of free expression.
- The incidental restriction on alleged First Amendment freedoms must be no greater than is essential to the furtherance of that interest.[101]

Clearly the Court gave freedom of speech a preferred position in the hierarchy of values. The Court declared that a government regulation could not withstand a constitutional challenge if the regulation directly sought to restrict free expression (*i.e.*, message content) for its own sake; also, a regulation unrelated to suppressing speech would be unconstitutional if its incidental impingement on freedom of speech was more than the minimum necessary to further the regulation's primary interest.

In the case of commercial speech, the Court arrived at a four-part test in *Central Hudson* that sought to emulate portions of *O'Brien*. The first prong of the test was actually a threshold requirement, that the speech concern lawful activity and not be misleading. The remaining three parts of *Central Hudson* may be contrasted with *O'Brien* above:

- The asserted governmental interest to be served by the restriction on commercial speech must be substantial.
- The regulation must directly advance the governmental interest asserted.
- The regulation must not be more extensive than necessary to serve that interest.[102]

In *S.U.N.Y.*, the last part of the test was weakened to say that the restriction must represent "a reasonable 'fit' between the government's ends and the means chosen to accomplish those ends,"[103] and expressly renounced the "least restrictive means" criterion of *Central Hudson*.

In light of this discussion let us return to the three hypotheses we posited earlier in considering commercial speech's relationship to First Amendment theory. (The three hypotheses again: (1) First Amendment theory properly excludes commercial speech; or (2) current theory is inadequate regarding commercial speech; or (3) we should forget theory in favor of values balancing.) We know that current First Amendment theory favors full protection for dignitary, self-expressive speech and for utilitarian speech of a political nature. We also know that under very limited circumstances, rights in these fully protected areas of speech may be minimally infringed when balanced against other substantial governmental interests. Thus we have a situation where a general theory of First Amendment protection is operable, yet is subject to occasional and extraordinary exceptions. In this area of traditional First Amendment protection, the fact that exceptions are sometimes called for does not make it necessary to do away with the theory entirely. For purposes of consistency, a decision arrived at as an exception to a rule is preferable to decisions arrived at without benefit of rules.

The same applies to commercial speech. *Central Hudson* and *S.U.N.Y.* have shown us the dangers of attempting to adjudicate questions of commercial speech strictly by trying to balance values as opposed to having a theory. To name two such dangers: free-speech rights for commercial speech can be (and have been) assigned a lower ranking than fully protected speech on the hierarchy of values, making commercial speech more susceptible to restrictions at the hands of competing values; and the rules by which the balancing game is played can be changed from case to case at the whim of the Court, as we saw in *S.U.N.Y.*

The fact that issues involving commercial speech are amorphous or difficult does not reduce the need for a theory. Nor does it mean that we must throw up our hands and declare that a theory would be futile because circumstances might require an occasional exception. That is precisely the situation in traditional First Amendment jurisprudence, and the system works well enough there. Lacking a general theory, however, commercial speech has been forced to rely on values balancing as the rule, rather than as an occasional exception to the rule. As Kozinski and Banner point out,[104] this has left us with a state of affairs in which:

> [G]overnment cannot prohibit certain sorts of commercial billboards,[105] but can prohibit the unauthorized use of certain words altogether.[106] Government cannot prohibit the mailing of unsolicited contraceptive advertisements,[107] but can prohibit advertisements for casino gambling.[108] Government cannot require professional fundraisers to obtain licenses,[109] but can prohibit college students from holding [housewares] parties in their dormitories.[110]

The inconsistent and unsatisfactory outcome of this approach is self evident and compels us to reject our third hypothesis. Likewise we reject our first hypothesis for reasons we shall develop in Chapter 5. This leaves us with our second hypothesis, that current First Amendment theory is inadequate in addressing commercial speech rights. This implies that a new theory needs to be formulated, and this is a task we shall begin to undertake also in Chapter 5. First, however, let us turn our attention to the other problem that vexes commercial speech and yet will be central to any workable theory: a definition of just what commercial speech is.

IV. Defining Commercial Speech

What are we talking about here, anyway? Or, to paraphrase an old pop standard, "What is this thing called commercial speech?" The answer is important for at least two reasons: Whether speech is defined as commercial or non-commercial determines whether the speech receives greater or lesser First Amendment protection—to define commercial speech is to distinguish it from fully protected non-commercial speech; second, a good definition is an important element in a workable theory of commercial speech protection—we have to be able to define what we want to protect.

Again let us begin our inquiry at the source, in this case the Supreme Court in *Valentine v. Chrestensen*.[111] The Court seemed remarkably untroubled by any definitional concerns, and referred only to "purely commercial advertising" without elaboration (the term "commercial speech" had yet to be coined). When in 1958 Justice Douglas referred to the *Valentine* decision as "casual, almost offhand,"[112] he noted that it dealt with "business advertisements and commercial matter,"— again with neither elaboration nor mention of commercial speech *per se*. The term can be found in the Court's 1973 ruling in *Pittsburgh*

Press,[113] which also introduced the standard definition of commercial speech. Referring to *Valentine*, the Court said the critical feature of Chrestensen's handbill was that "it *did no more than propose a commercial transaction*, the sale of admission to a submarine (emphasis added)."[114] That definition stuck, and we are still stuck with it today. The Court suggested an additional definition in *Central Hudson* in 1980: "expression related solely to the economic interests of the speaker and its audience."[115] This was synthesized from some things the Court had said along the way: "[W]e may assume that the advertiser's interest is a purely economic one" (*Virginia Pharmacy Board*),[116] and the somewhat broader "largely economic" interest it had noted in *Bates v. State Bar of Arizona*.[117]

Over the years the Court gave more clues to the meaning of commercial speech by describing what it was not. In *New York Times Co. v. Sullivan* it said the fact that a speaker pays to project a message does not make the message commercial speech—that paying for an ad "is as immaterial . . . as is the fact that books and newspapers are sold."[118] The Court noted that paid advertising is an "important outlet" for people "who wish to exercise their freedom of speech even though they are not members of the press."[119]

In *Virginia Pharmacy Board* the Court cited, in addition to *Sullivan*, examples of speech that is fully protected even though an economic dimension is involved:

> Speech likewise is protected even though it is carried in a form that is "sold" for profit, *Smith v. California*, 361 U.S. 147, 150 (1959) (books); *Joseph Burstyn, Inc. v. Wilson*, 343 U.S. 495, 501 (1952) (motion pictures); *Murdock v. Pennsylvania*, 319 U.S., at 111 (religious literature), and even though it may involve a solicitation to purchase or otherwise pay or contribute money. *New York Times Co. v. Sullivan, supra*; *NAACP v. Button*, 371 U.S. 415, 429 (1963); *Jamison v. Texas*, 318 U.S. at 417; *Cantwell v. Connecticut*, 310 U.S. 296, 306-307 (1940).[120]

The Court went on to say that even an advertiser's "purely economic" interest "hardly disqualifies him from protection under the

First Amendment," citing a number of labor-relations cases.[121] In *S.U.N.Y.* the Court distinguished commercial speech from speech uttered for a profit—it classed job counseling, tutoring, legal advice, and medical consultation provided for a fee in dormitory rooms as non-commercial because such speech did not *propose* a commercial transaction.[122] And in *First National Bank of Boston v. Bellotti*,[123] the Court ruled that corporations were capable of non-commercial speech, in this case political: "We thus find no support in the First or Fourteenth Amendment, or in the decisions of this Court, for the proposition that speech that otherwise would be within the protection of the First Amendment loses that protection simply because its source is a corporation. . . ."[124]

Advertising Content. The current necessity of defining commercial v. non-commercial speech introduces the significant problem of trying to classify speech that contains both proposals of transactions and purely informational elements. The Court has wrestled with this problem, and its range of interpretations testifies to the difficulty of the task. In *Valentine* the Court held that protected speech forfeited its protection if it appeared with commercial speech: "[E]very merchant who desires to broadcast advertising leaflets in the streets need only append a civic appeal, or a moral platitude, to achieve immunity from the law's command."[125] In *Bigelow* the Court took a more expansive approach and said that because the ad in question "contained factual material of clear 'public interest,'" it was an exercise of free speech in which the "appellant's First Amendment interests coincided with the constitutional interests of the general public."[126] But the Court retreated in 1983 when it evaluated pamphlets that discussed prophylactics, and the availability of a certain brand. In *Bolger v. Youngs Drug Products Corp.* the Court concluded that the pamphlets were in fact commercial speech, and were not entitled to full protection even though they attempted to link a product to a current public debate.[127]

Two noteworthy cases in this regard involved the Federal Trade Commission. In *National Commission on Egg Nutrition v. FTC*,[128] the U.S. Court of Appeals for the Seventh Circuit held that an ad which denied the existence of scientific evidence about the ill effects of eating eggs was commercial speech. The egg group argued that its ads should be entitled to First Amendment protection because they were commenting on an important public issue and did not propose a commercial transaction. But the court disagreed and interpreted commercial speech doctrine as extending "to false claims as to the harmlessness of the advertiser's product asserted for the purpose of persuading members of the reading public to buy the product."[129] As commercial speech that was deemed to be misleading, the ads were without First Amendment protection and subject to the regulatory authority of the FTC, which the court upheld.

An administrative law judge reached a different conclusion in *In re R.J. Reynolds Tobacco Co.*[130] The company had published an advertisement that discussed a particular scientific study and concluded, based on the study's findings, that "the controversy over smoking and health remains an open one." The FTC claimed the ad was false and misleading and might cause the public to underestimate the health problems associated with smoking. Using a commonsense approach, the judge concluded that the ad was an editorial and thus a form of protected speech. He noted that it did not contain "*express* promotional language," did not mention a specific product as in *Bolger*, and did not make the type of claims found in the egg council ad. The matter was reversed and remanded, but after protracted procedural wranglings Reynolds entered a consent decree with the FTC that did not admit any violations but agreed not to misrepresent the study's results in future ads.

As this brief overview suggests, the distinction between commercial and non-commercial speech is not easily discerned. Commercial speech traditionally refers to advertising, but we know that non-commercial speech may be conveyed via ads. The commercial identity of the speech is not decisive: Corporations may engage in both commercial and non-commercial speech. Nor is the economic incentive of the speaker a determining factor: An ad that seeks to enhance the speaker's profits by proposing the sale of his goods is commercial speech, but the stories appearing in a newspaper that is published to enhance its owner's profits are non-commercial. An ad that proposes a commercial transaction is commercial speech if it is selling a product, but not if the sale is in the form of a contribution for which the recipient receives a religious trinket. And speech proposing a transaction may or may not be commercial depending on the extent to which it also includes information of general public interest.

Some Examples. As a practical matter, the guidelines the Court has given us make it almost impossible to tell the difference between commercial and non-commercial speech once we move beyond the simplest examples. Perhaps the paradigm example of speech that does "no more than propose a commercial transaction" is the weekly supermarket ad in the newspaper that consists entirely of listings of items on sale and prices, with a few illustrations of product packages or brand names. Glossy inserts for discount stores, home improvement stores, and department stores can be placed in the same category.

What about product ads that don't propose a transaction? A television spot for KitchenAid appliances shows a day in the life of an older couple as they prepare for a big family reunion, perhaps to celebrate their anniversary. They're busy with food preparations. . .the family arrives. . .they enjoy the celebration with toasts and hugs. . .and at the end of the day they enjoy each other's company alone in the kitchen as they clean up. This ad is a little piece of art, the type of artistic expression we usually think of as meriting First Amendment protection. The couple's day—starting out together/family arriving/fun with family/family departing/couple alone at end—is a microcosm of their married life together. It's the kind of "feel good" ad that could just as easily end with a tagline for Kodak or Hallmark Cards. During it all a singer croons "Through the years, you've never let me down. . . ." Is this what the husband in the commercial, now in his twilight years, is thinking about his devoted wife—or about their KitchenAid dishwasher? The ad doesn't ask us to buy KitchenAid appliances, so we must assume this is what the manufacturer is implying. But that supposes a motive on the manufacturer's part, something we are not allowed to consider in determining whether the speech is commercial. Intuitively we know this is commercial speech, yet strictly speaking it falls outside the scope of commercial speech as currently defined.

Consider this: Texaco runs an ad to announce that the Metropolitan Opera is staging a new Zeffirelli production of Mozart's "Don Giovanni," and that Texaco is sponsoring a PBS broadcast of this at a certain date and time. The ad invites the reader to view the program, but neither mentions Texaco products nor asks the reader to do anything except watch the TV show. Is Texaco running this ad (and sponsoring the show) merely as a public service, or does it hope to create a favorable impression of Texaco among those who see the ad—and who presumably buy gasoline more often than they attend the opera? What about the black-bordered ad in the *Wall Street Journal* that mourns the passing of the XYZ Company's founder, and mentions at the bottom that the XYZ Company is a manufacturer of precision valves and fittings? Is that last line a factual piece of information of interest to the general public, or a subtle inducement for readers in the market for valves and fittings to consider the XYZ Company? The list is endless, and others have offered excellent examples of how the current definition of commercial speech has led to a breakdown of the distinctions between commercial and artistic speech, commercial and scientific speech, commercial and political speech, and commercial and religious speech.[131]

Other Characteristics. We have reached a point, then, when the Court's definition of commercial speech is so out of step with the realities of current advertising practices that our judgments can be arrived at more accurately by intuition. Are there any other characteristics possessed by commercial speech alone that would distinguish it from non-commercial speech? As it happens, the Court has noted two such qualities, and commentators a third.

In a footnote in *Virginia Pharmacy Board*, the Court alluded to the "commonsense differences" between commercial speech and other varieties which, the Court said, had to do with commercial speech's greater objectivity and durability:

> The truth of commercial speech, for example, may be more easily verifiable by its disseminator than, let us say, news reporting or political commentary, in that ordinarily the

advertiser seeks to disseminate information about a specific product or service that he himself provides and presumably knows more about than anyone else. Also, commercial speech may be more durable than other kinds. Since advertising is the *sine qua non* of commercial profits, there is little likelihood of its being chilled by proper regulation and forgone entirely.[132]

The Court concluded that "[a]ttributes such as these, the greater objectivity and hardiness of commercial speech, may make it less necessary to tolerate inaccurate statements for fear of silencing the speaker."[133] For the sake of argument let's accept for a moment the Court's assertion that commercial speech is more objective and durable, and see where that leads. The Court has at last identified a reason for regulating commercial speech more strictly: Because commercial speech is motivated by profit (perhaps we could call this profit-seeking speech), it can be beat over the head harder and longer by government but it will keep coming back more tenaciously than other types of non-profit-seeking speech. Presumably, then, the profit motive is so overwhelming that speech in search of profits is uttered with a forcefulness and conviction that cannot be approached by other types of speech. Of course we know this to be false—we need look no further than the speech emanating from the civil-rights movement or from both sides of the abortion issue to realize that great fervor can be attached to speech not connected with profit seeking. (The same can be said of religious speech, provided one is wary of including the so-called televangelists as examples of fervent speakers with motives wholly apart from profit seeking.)

Regarding objectivity, if the Court believes a stricter level of regulation is appropriate because commercial speech is more objective, this is another way of saying that commercial speech should be regulated more strictly just because it is easier to regulate than other types of speech. But this is only a convenience argument, and doesn't address whether it is right to restrict commercial speech for any substantive reason. Many other types of speech are easy to regulate (such as prohibiting public anti-war protests) yet we tolerate them for other reasons. Moreover, advertising is known to employ hyperbole, to associate products with certain feelings, and to create images—outcomes that are not inherently objective or subject to quantification. At the same time, other types of protected speech, such as scientific speech, are highly objective and verifiable. Others have made these points and offered more examples, so we will not belabor the issue here except to state an important observation: Even if commercial speech were more objective and durable (which it is not), these are still not reasons to treat commercial speech differently than other types of speech.

Thus far we have been unable to distinguish anything about commercial speech that would make it a candidate for reduced First Amendment protection, based on what the Court has told us. Blanket definitions have proved inadequate, and the characteristics the Court has identified such as objectivity and durability have been shown to be flawed. Either there is in fact no distinction, or we (and the Court) have missed something.

The answer may be the latter. In an incisive analysis, Daniel A. Farber suggests that the distinguishing characteristic of commercial speech is its contractual nature. He notes that a commercial speaker not only talks about a product, but also sells it, and that the sale itself is subject to regulations that include the attachment of liability to the sale's contract language. Advertising, he argues, induces the potential buyer to enter into a transaction based on the express or implied promises the ad makes. This contractual function of advertising is distinct from its informative function, and from the informative function of fully protected speech. "The unique aspect of commercial speech is that it is a prelude to, and therefore becomes integrated into, a contract, the essence of which is the presence of a promise,"[134] he says. Farber emphasizes the dual nature of commercial speech as something both contractual and informative:

> Similar to the language of a written contract, the language in advertising can be seen as constituting part of the seller's commitment to the buyer. Thus, advertising can function as part of the contractual arrangement between the buyer and seller. Of course, in addition to serving this contractual

function, advertisements also serve an informative function to which the first amendment applies. The critical factor seems to be whether a state rule is based on the informative function or the contractual function of the language.[135]

Focusing on the contractual nature of commercial speech may begin to solve some of the perplexing definitional problems we have been encountering. Farber offers a definition that is a good start:

> In addition to being a means of conveying information, commercial speech is also a means of forming commitments which are potentially part of the contract of sale.[136]

This definition has several advantages: It recognizes that commercial speech often conveys information in addition to proposing a transaction; it encompasses a broad range of advertising (like our KitchenAid example) that evades the *Pittsburgh Press* definition because such ads hope to induce favorable consumer action but do not propose a transaction outright; and it isolates only that portion of commercial speech—the contractual portion—that is appropriate for some degree of government concern.

One of the definitional problems we have faced: The Court has sought to define commercial speech not only to distinguish it from other types of speech (much as it may be helpful to distinguish artistic from religious expression), but also to provide a justification for affording it less First Amendment protection. This has proved an impossible task for what now becomes an obvious reason: All speech that does nothing more than propose a commercial transaction is contractual in nature, but this contractual nature is also found in a far wider range of speech that does not propose specific transactions— therefore the definition fails because it falls short of capturing the range of speech it seeks.

The traditional definition also fails because it neglects to recognize that commercial speech may possess an informative nature in addition to a contractual one. The *Central Hudson* attempt to remedy this, by defining commercial speech as "expression related solely to the economic interests of the speaker and its audience," also fails because it is too broad and would submit to stricter scrutiny far more than the contractual aspects of commercial speech.

The same reasons that have made it impossible for the Court to find a suitable definition have also made it impossible for the Court to offer a compelling argument as to why commercial speech deserves less protection. (We reject as not compelling all "commonsense" arguments.) The problem has been the Court's insistence on linking the defining of commerical speech to the limiting of protection. To define commercial speech heretofore has meant to limit First Amendment rights for the entire category of speech, however it is defined. But commercial speech often contains much information that is already protected, and still more that should be protected for reasons we will develop in the next chapter.

What we are left with is a subset of commercial speech—only the part that is contractual in nature. This appears to be the subset that the Court has been trying to define unsuccessfully as the whole of the commercial speech category. And it appears that this contractual subset is really what the Court has in mind when it says that commercial speech is deserving of less First Amendment protection. It is only this subset that deserves less protection, if by this we mean that *contractual* language that is false or misleading should be judged according to stricter standards (such as Section 43(a) of the Lanham Act or contract law generally).

We have not yet solved the definitional problem (although Farber gives us a good start) but we have made a key distinction: However we define commercial speech as a category, we can do so without worrying that our definition will subject the entire category to a stricter standard of review. In one sense our definition will be more for our convenience in classifying a category of speech, than for demarcating a line below which all speech is automatically stripped of full First Amendment protection. Only contractual language that is false or misleading would trigger stricter review, and would be excluded from First Amendment protection. We shall keep these parameters in mind as we return in the next chapter to our consideration of a new theory of commercial speech.

V. A Reasonable Approach for Extending First Amendment Rights to Commercial Speech

Thus far we have seen that commercial speech, in its 50-year sojourn through American jurisprudence, has had a distinctly checkered history *vis-à-vis* the First Amendment. Commercial speech doctrine was conceived in a manner that was "casual, almost offhand," and has been guided for too long by "commonsense" assumptions about why commercial speech is supposedly inferior to other types of protected expression.

Commercial speech has, in large measure, existed in a theoretical vacuum, somehow unable to become integrated into broader First Amendment theory—we can speculate whether the intuitive approach that has evolved is a cause or an effect of this theoretical void. The problem has been compounded by the difficulty in arriving at an acceptable definition; commercial speech definitions have not only had to define a category of speech, but have carried the additional burden of limiting First Amendment protection for the entire category of speech they define.

As a result of this rather *ad hoc* situation, First Amendment protection for commercial speech has been eroding gradually since its

high point in *Virginia Pharmacy Board* in 1976. This erosion needs
to be stopped for the sake of a strong First Amendment and for the
sake of an informed citizenry. Toward this end we would offer some
observations on why a theoretical basis does in fact exist for extending full First Amendment rights to commercial speech, and what this
might mean in practice.

A word about an underlying assumption: This discussion will
assume that a theory-based approach to the issue can be workable.
The theoretical framework envisioned has two pillars: (1) the primacy
of the First Amendment generally and as applied to commercial
speech; and (2) a rejection of values balancing as an end in itself.
This recognizes freedom of speech as a primary value that aspires
to be absolute, and is more than a "common value" that the state can
barter away routinely in exchange for other values it may favor. This
also acknowledges, however, that in extreme circumstances balancing First Amendment values against competing values may be inevita-
ble, in which cases a strict First Amendment test like *O'Brien* should
be in order.

We begin with a proposition that we believe to be as true as it is
unambiguous:

> Truthful speech about lawful products and activities should
> receive full First Amendment protection.

The obvious question is why. The answer centers on the importance of economic information to the individual listener and to the
functioning of the economy. In actual life, and perhaps at some remove
from judicial chambers and the groves of academe, economic information *has* achieved parity with political information. Justice Blackmun recognized that economic information may in fact be *more*
important to the average citizen:

> As to the particular consumer's interest in the free flow of
> commercial information, that interest may be as keen, if not
> keener by far, than his interest in the day's most urgent polit-
> ical debate.[137]

Nor is this a condition that has sprung up overnight. Aaron Director, known for his pioneering work in the law and economics movement, took note of this phenomenon in the mid-1960s:

> [T]he bulk of mankind will for the foreseeable future have to devote a considerable fraction of their active lives to economic activity. For these people freedom of choice as owners of resources in choosing within available and continually changing opportunities, areas of employment, investment, and consumption is fully as important as freedom of discussion and participation in government.[138]

Some commentators dismiss the economic parity argument, but they do so by setting up an apples-and-oranges comparison. An ad for the deodorants on sale at Brown's Pharmacy does not deserve the same First Amendment protection as a discourse on the merits of democratic v. totalitarian government, the argument goes. But it compares the mundane with the lofty. Should we not be asking if the treatise on government merits more protection than information on capital formation or asset allocation strategies? Conversely, does the pharmacy flier deserve less protection than a flier that says "Vote for Bill Smith—City Council"? In the latter case both fliers are mundane attempts to induce the recipient to make a choice—but for our average citizen the choice of deodorant may well have greater import for his daily life than his choice of city council member.

There may be another bias against the economic parity argument. Many commentators who question parity are political scientists or law professors who have invested a great deal of their personal and professional lives in the idea that the study of politics and government is the loftiest of intellectual pursuits. Perhaps the parity argument would be embraced more widely if economists were better represented among the commentators.

So far we have argued that economic information in its own right enjoys parity with political information. We can also argue that economic information has become so entwined with political information that it is impossible to separate the two. It has become a bit of common wisdom, for instance, that presidential elections have become referenda on the state of the economy. Almost every political debate involves questions about the formation or allocation of resources. Should taxes be raised? How much should government spend on social programs and how much should the private sector bear? Can the government afford to bail out the savings-and-loans? Are we spending too much or too little on defense? Are these political or economic questions?

The above observations suggest a handy syllogism: Economic concerns are as important to our society as political concerns. By extension, economic information is as important as political information. Political information receives full First Amendment protection. Therefore, economic information should receive full First Amendment protection. (This will have the effect of protecting much economic expression that is mundane, like our deodorant ad, but we already protect much political expression that is equally mundane such as campaign speeches.)

Our syllogism leaves a key question unanswered: Why do we protect political speech? In Chapter 3 we identified two reasons: for its dignitary value and for its utilitarian value. Political speech has dignitary value when it is uttered by an individual as a form of personal expression. The act of speaking on a political topic is a manifestation of the individual's human dignity, which can also be manifested through artistic or religious self-expression.

But we are concerned here with the utilitarian value of political speech—that is, its value to listeners in allowing them to make informed choices about their government. Our democratic system works on the basis of individual choice; the availability of political information facilitates these choices and leads to the efficient operation of the system. The same is true of our economic system—this too is choice based and depends on individuals making economic decisions. These are more likely to be in individuals' best interests if they are informed choices, and this is the important role that commercial speech plays. It enhances the quality of economic choice that an individual is able to make, and facilitates the efficient operation of the wider economy. The Court, in fact, recognized this in *Bates*: "[C]ommercial speech serves to inform the public of the availability, nature, and prices o products and services, and thus performs an indispensable role in the allocation of resources in a free enterprise system."[139]

Returning to our syllogism, we can say that since political speech receives full First Amendment protection because of its utilitarian value to the governing process, commercial speech should receive full First Amendment protection because of its utilitarian value to the equally important economic process.

This leads us in the direction of First Amendment theory that is listener centered. The Court has recognized in numerous decisions since at least the 1940s[140] that the listener, as well as the speaker, has a First Amendment right in the speech being conveyed. In *Kleindienst v. Mandel* the Court referred to a First Amendment right to "receive information and ideas," and noted that freedom of speech " 'necessarily protects the right to receive.' "[141] In *Red Lion Broadcasting Co. v. FCC* the Court stated that "[i]t is the right of the viewers and listeners, not the right of the broadcasters which is paramount."[142] The Court addressed the rights of listeners in the context of commercial speech in *Virginia Pharmacy Board* when it noted that "the protection afforded is to the communication, to its source and to its recipients both," and that "[i]f there is a right to advertise, there is a reciprocal right to receive the advertising. . . ."[143]

This listener-based right evolved because the Court encountered a number of cases in which there was no individual speaker with a dignitary interest. In *Lamont v. Postmaster General*,[144] for instance, the "speaker" was a foreign government that mailed propaganda papers to a U.S. citizen. In *Procunier v. Martinez*[145] it was a felon who had lost his own First Amendment protection; in other cases the speakers were corporations that, as collectives chartered by the state, lacked the capacity for human self-expression. In order to extend First Amendment protection to their speech, the Court invested the listener with the right to receive the speech. In turn the speaker was essentially able to "borrow back" the right of the listener, and that became the speaker's interest in providing the information. In other words, the speaker was not asserting a dignitary interest of its own in the speech (because it was not entitled to a dignitary interest, for whatever reason); rather, the speaker was asserting the listener's interest in receiving the speech.

These circumstances in the political realm led to the development of the utilitarian branch of First Amendment theory. There has been some confusion in trying to apply the commercial speech example to political speech because political speech can be either dignitary (if uttered by an individual for self-expression) or utilitarian (uttered for the benefit of the listener). Commercial speech generally cannot be dignitary in nature because advertisers tend to be corporations without the capacity for dignitary self-expression. Some commentators erroneously stop here in asserting that commercial speech is not entitled to First Amendment protection.

However, commercial speech strongly implicates the rights of listeners, and thus is wonderfully analogous to political speech in the utilitarian branch of First Amendment theory. In fact, the contractual nature of commercial speech *requires* a listener—the other party to the potential contract—as a part of its nature. The commercial speaker has no reason to propose a transaction in the absence of a listener who might respond to that proposal. In this utilitarian framework, then, First Amendment rights for commercial speech reside totally with the listener, and are "borrowed back" by the commercial speaker. But these rights exist just as surely and just as strongly for commercial speech as they do for political speech of a utilitarian nature. The (utilitarian) political speaker and the commercial speaker both derive their First Amendment rights from the utilitarian value of their speech to their listeners. Both types of speech deserve equal First Amendment protection.

Objections examined. Critics fear that bad things will happen if full First Amendment rights for commercial speech are recognized, and two are cited most often: a dilution of free-speech rights for other types of protected expression, and the wholesale abandonment of mechanisms for combating consumer fraud. These fears are misplaced because the chances of either happening are remote indeed.

Regarding dilution, there are critics who feel that the First Amendment has gotten out of hand, and that it already protects too many kinds of expression that are frivolous, morally insidious, or even unpatriotic to the point of threatening the Republic. To them, commercial speech is just one more competitor in a zero-sum game that has already gone too far: If commercial speech gets more First Amendment protection, traditional protected speech will receive that much less—or at least that will be the effect, they fear, since raising the level of protection for commercial speech reduces the "protection gap" between it and traditional speech.

But the dilution argument fails for at least two reasons. First, the types of speech these critics decry as already going too far are almost always dignitary types of self-expression, such as artistic and aesthetic speech (and political speech that is dignitary—as opposed to utilitarian—in the case of flag burners). The extent to which these types of speech should be protected engages a whole different set of concerns that are appropriate in the consideration of dignitary speech. Commercial speech is a different ballgame—it is utilitarian in nature, and thus must be judged by different criteria as we have done. (And the judgment, as we have attempted to show, is resoundingly in favor of full First Amendment rights.)

Second, freedom of speech is not a zero-sum game and raising the protection for one category of speech does not diminish the protection granted to another. To suggest an analogy: If your net worth is $5 million and I, your next-door neighbor, have a net worth of $1 million, you do not become poorer (*i.e.*, worth less than $5 million) because I score on some investments and raise my net worth to $5 million. You may *feel* poorer, because we now have economic parity, but you certainly have not sacrificed any of your net worth to enhance mine. And so it is with freedom of speech. In fact, just the opposite is likely to happen, as demonstrated in the case that opened this Pandora's box. Our friend Chrestensen was prohibited from conveying his political protest about the New York City docks precisely because the commercial portion of his message (the invitation to purchase a ticket to tour his submarine) was not protected. In this instance the presence of unprotected commercial speech wiped out the protection for political speech.

Regarding consumer protection, critics raise the spectre of fraud statutes being wiped off the books if commercial speech is fully protected; the government will be powerless to stop false and misleading advertising claims, they say. Under our proposal, however, critics need not fear. Consumers would still be protected because commercial speech's contractual language that proved false or misleading would still be subject to regulations that met the *O'Brien* test. Others have already suggested how this would work in the case of consumer fraud statutes that prohibit false representations about products:

> Would the statute unconstitutionally abridge the freedom of speech? Prevention of consumer fraud is unquestionably a substantial governmental interest; even the most ardent libertarians agree that it is a legitimate role of government to prevent citizens from cheating one another. The governmental interest is unrelated to the suppression of expression; the seller is free to say whatever he likes about the product, true or not, as long as he doesn't induce sales in reliance on what he says. And last, it should not be difficult to tailor a fraud statute narrowly to suppress no more speech than is necessary. Extending full protection to commercial speech, despite dire predictions from some quarters, will not give free rein to unscrupulous salesmen.[146]

The likely outcome, in fact, may be closer to having the best of both worlds: full protection for commercial speech that serves to reinforce the protections for political speech, while safeguarding consumers against fraud.

Final Thoughts: A Prescription for Action[147]

Commercial speech doctrine has existed for 50 years, but for only four of those years has the doctrine favored a properly expansive concept of First Amendment rights—the "Golden Age" that began with *Virginia Pharmacy Board* in 1976 and ended with *Central Hudson* in 1980. The interval from *Central Hudson* until *Posadas* in 1986 was not the best of times, but it was not the worst of times either. The

Court had retreated from *Virginia Pharmacy Board* but had constructed a balancing test that afforded some protection to commercial speech. Unfortunately the situation since *Posadas* has been unpredictable and shows signs of getting worse absent a rethinking of commercial speech doctrine. That has been the aim of this publication, to share the thoughts of this author and of knowledgeable commentators with a wider audience as a starting point in rethinking commercial speech doctrine. If the situation is to improve, that is, if the First Amendment is to be strengthened rather than weakened, some changes need to occur: in judicial thinking, and in the actions of regulators and legislators who have proved themselves far too eager to provoke constitutional mischief.

Our prescription for action begins, then, by summarizing the doctrinal aspects we have discussed earlier—the aspects that are critical in any rethinking of commercial speech by the judiciary. Our prescription goes beyond the theoretical and extends to the actions of regulators and legislators, and suggests some strong medicine that they will, no doubt, find unpalatable.

1. *Reassert the primacy of the First Amendment and recognize the distinction between dignitary and utilitarian speech.*
   Freedom of speech should be approached as an absolute value, even if we know that it is not always possible to treat it that way in a society of competing values. By giving it a position of primacy we will encourage a consistency of judicial opinion (and, we can hope, a consistency of regulatory and legislative action) that cannot be guaranteed if we balance freedom of speech against other values on a case-by-case basis. An observation by Justice Stewart in 1973 is every bit as prescient today: "So long as Members of this Court view the First Amendment as no more than a set of 'values' to be balanced against other 'values,' that Amendment will remain in grave jeopardy."[148] In cases where competing values unavoidably result in regulations that conflict with the First Amendment, those regulations should be given strict scrutiny according to tests such as *O'Brien*. At the same time we need to recognize that freedom of speech embraces two distinct types of expression—

dignitary speech (reflecting the speaker's worth as a human being) that encompasses literary, artistic, aesthetic, religious, and political self-expression; and utilitarian speech (deriving its value from its importance to the listener) that encompasses political and economic speech.

2. *Extend full First Amendment rights to commercial speech based on its utilitarian value, which is equal to that of political speech.* The Founders recognized that the free flow of political information is critical in a democracy, because information allows citizens to make informed choices about their government. In modern society economic information is equally important, and may in fact be more important to the average citizen. Economic information (*i.e.*, commercial speech in its popular embodiment) plays a role in the economy that is equal to the role played by political information in the governing process. Political speech, of course, has received constitutional protection for its utilitarian value to the listener/political decisionmaker since colonial days. Because commercial speech has the same or greater utilitarian value to the listener/economic decisionmaker, it too should receive the same constitutional protection. At a practical level this suggests that the Supreme Court should abandon the *Central Hudson* test and instead judge regulations that threaten the First Amendment rights of commercial speech according to *O'Brien*, the test used in connection with other types of protected speech.

3. *Work toward defining commercial speech in a way that recognizes its unique contractual nature.*
   The Court's *Pittsburgh Press* and *Central Hudson* definitions have been too narrow and too broad, respectively, and both have failed to apprehend the unique contractual aspect of commercial speech, which may extend well beyond the proposal of a specific transaction. As a start (and only a start to be sure) let us suggest a new definition:

> Commercial speech is speech that proposes a commer-
> cial transaction or forms commitments that are poten-
> tially part of future transactions.

This definition employs the idea of proposing a transaction from *Pittsburgh Press*, and borrows heavily from Farber's concept of commercial speech as contractual in nature. Actually, the need to define commercial speech loses much of its urgency under the doctrinal proposals we are suggesting here. Our new definition need serve only one function: describing a category of speech. It need no longer serve the additional function of limiting First Amendment protection for the speech it describes. If commercial speech receives full First Amendment protection, it no longer matters as much where we draw the line between it and other types of protected speech—they're all protected one way or another. We no longer need a definition to tell us whether the speech in question should be subject to regulations that meet the *Central Hudson* test or, in the alternative, the *O'Brien* test. If commercial speech is fully protected the *O'Brien* test alone will suffice. Still, it is nice to be able to describe what we are talking about, so we offer the definition above as a strawman in that endeavor.

4. *Maintain federal preemption of state regulation of national advertising, and keep regulatory authority for national advertising vested in the Federal Trade Commission.*

The best doctrine the courts can apply comes too late if First Amendment rights have already been impinged by overzealous regulators. "The loss of First Amendment freedoms, for even minimal periods of time, unquestionably constitutes irreparable injury," the Supreme Court has said.[149] A disturbing trend in this direction has been the movement by state attorneys general to proclaim authority to regulate national advertising appearing in their states. Recent legislative proposals would even allow local regulation of cigarette advertising. Such initiatives may further the regulatory agendas of state and local officials, but these agendas are unconcerned with—and even seem to flaunt—their impact on freedom of speech. Even if an *O'Brien* test found most of their regulations overbroad (as no doubt it would), the courts would face an unnecessary overload, commercial speech would be chilled as advertisers found the burden of compliance too heavy, and the public would be denied much useful information that is essential to economic decisionmaking.

National advertising can be overseen quite effectively by the Federal Trade Commission. But here too a word of caution is in order. Over the years the FTC has, at times, been moved by regulatory zeal to exceed constitutional bounds. The *O'Brien* test would be a good check on FTC regulation, but again could come too late in the process to help many advertisers—and not at all for advertisers who give up the fight and find it more expedient to enter consent decrees.

If we could make only one recommendation to the FTC, we would suggest that the Commission err on the side of too much, rather than too little, information reaching the public. This is especially relevant in the area of health claims made for food products. In substantiating such claims the FTC attempts to discern the consensus of scientists having expertise in the pertinent area. But, as we have seen in too many cases, scientific opinion changes over time as new information comes to light. Cyclamates were banned as cancer-causing agents in 1969, but recent studies indicate the danger was grossly exaggerated. Government warnings on the danger of salt consumption have proved too broad, as later evidence has shown that salt is a significant factor in raising blood pressure only among a very small percentage of the population that is so predisposed; salt is by no means a health threat to the general population.

The danger, then, is that the FTC can regulate the flow of speech based on scientific evidence that is incomplete or simply inaccurate. This is bad from the standpoint of First Amendment freedom, and is also detrimental to the interests of consumers. Then-FTC Chairman Miller noted in 1984 that consumers can be hurt both if the FTC requires too little substantiation (because they may fall prey to false claims) and by *too much* substantiation (because this reduces the flow of useful, truthful information).[150] The director of the

Commission's Bureau of Consumer Protection noted that too much substantiation would "deny people the opportunity to gain truthful information that may be important to them . . . .[T]he folly of the overly stringent approach is apparent."[151]

While the FTC's goal of restricting false and misleading advertising is appropriate, the task must be undertaken in a way that is mindful of the shortcomings of scientific data. The FTC should worry more about encouraging the free flow of information to consumers, and less about creating a paternalistic, zero-risk environment.

5. *Remind the U.S. Congress and state legislatures that they have an obligation to act in accord with the Constitution.*

The federal and state legislatures have been among the worst offenders in flaunting First Amendment rights. Legislative proposals, especially those to ban or restrict advertising for consumer products, display a blatant disregard for the constitutional interest in assuring a free flow of information. The political process is essentially a values-balancing process. But as we have seen, that approach is inadequate where the First Amendment is concerned—it is not merely one more value to be traded away. Somehow legislators must be made aware that freedom of speech is a constitutionally protected right, and that First Amendment rights necessarily extend to commercial speech. If legislators find certain products to be undesirable (alcohol and tobacco come to mind, but the list is virtually endless), and if they wish the public to reduce its consumption of such products, these lawmakers should address their legislative initiatives to the conduct itself (*i.e.*, the buying and consuming of the product) and not to the speech surrounding the product. The Court has traditionally held that the regulation of conduct is preferable to the regulation of speech; legislators would do well to heed this maxim, to stop taking easy political shots at advertising, and to let their deliberations be guided by the primacy of the First Amendment.

6. *Challenge those who are indifferent to commercial speech protection—especially consumer activists and even certain First Amendment advocates—to recognize that the constitutional aspects of commercial speech cannot be ignored without imperiling the First Amendment itself.*

People who are motivated to do good would do well to remember that advertising is a form of speech deserving First Amendment protection. Restricting advertising cannot, therefore, be viewed as merely one more means of trying to solve social problems, no matter how pressing they may seem. Let us assume for a moment that advertising restrictions and bans could be effective at reducing consumption of disfavored products (even though the evidence on this point is inconclusive at best). The fact that a ban might be effective does not amount to a principled reason to employ it—not if one aspires to the principle that freedom of speech should be treated as an absolute value. Trying to solve one problem, such as alcohol abuse, by restricting advertising only creates the bigger problem of damage to the First Amendment. Ways to deal with social problems must be found that do not trample the constitutional right to freedom of speech. What is needed generally is a greater awareness, even among those who otherwise advocate a strong First Amendment, of the rightful place of commercial speech in the constitutional scheme of things.

●   ●   ●

First Amendment protection for commercial speech is at a crossroads. It has reached this point because legislators and regulators, with the acquiescence and even enthusiasm of a public that is indifferent to commercial speech protection, seem more zealous than ever in advancing restrictions on advertising that would be blatantly unconstitutional if applied to other forms of expression. Meanwhile the Supreme Court, having adopted a case-by-case approach for deciding commercial speech questions, seems more unpredictable as a check on regulatory excess. This is so because the Court has allowed commercial speech doctrine to evolve for 50 years without benefit of a theoretical justification that has been soundly reasoned and consistently applied. The situation has been further muddied by the difficulty in defining commercial speech adequately. If commercial speech case law continues on this *ad hoc* course, the only prediction we can make with certainty is that First Amendment protection for commercial speech will continue to diminish; there is no reason to expect consistent improvement.

But this need not be the case, and indeed should not be the case. As we have attempted to show here, a sound justification already exists in First Amendment jurisprudence for full free-speech rights—the utilitarian value of commercial speech to the listener. The time has come for the Supreme Court and lower courts to rethink commercial speech doctrine—in light, we would hope, of the arguments made here and elsewhere. The time has also come for federal and state regulators and legislators to recognize the primacy of the First Amendment—and the rightful place of commercial speech therein—and to act accordingly.

Truthful speech about lawful products and services deserves full First Amendment protection. This is a simple proposition, but its implications for freedom of speech extend far beyond advertising. It is time for our jurists, legislators, and regulators to embrace this proposition—for in so doing they will be reaffirming that freedom of speech is indeed a basic tenet of our democracy.

Notes

Chapter 1

[1] *Olmstead v. U.S.*, 277 U.S. 438, 479 (1928)(Brandeis, L., dissenting).

[2] *See Virginia State Board of Pharmacy v. Virginia Citizens Consumer Council, infra* note 30, and *Central Hudson Gas & Electric Corp. v. Public Service Comm'n of New York, infra* note 39.

[3] *Posadas de Puerto Rico Assoc's v. Tourism Co. of Puerto Rico, infra* note 48.

[4] *Board of Trustees of the State Univ. of New York v. Fox, infra* note 56.

[5] *Peel v. Attorney Registration and Disciplinary Comm'n of Illinois, infra* note 78.

[6] Crawford, Carol, "Remarks before the American Advertising Federation," Dec. 4, 1984, at 12-13.

[7] *Trans World Airlines v. Mattox*, 897 F.2d 773 (5th Cir. 1990).

[8] Federal Trade Commission Act, 15 U.S.C. §45.

[9] *Central Hudson Gas & Electric Corp. v. Public Service Comm'n of New York*, *infra* note 39.

[10] Trade Reg. Rep. (CCH) ¶50,455 (1983).

[11] *Policy Statement Regarding Advertising Substantiation Program*, 49 Fed. Reg. 30,999 (1984).

[12] *Bureau of Consumer Protection, Advertising Substantiation Program, Analysis of Public Comments and Recommended Changes*, July 23, 1984, at 31 and n. 60.

[13] *Peel v. Attorney Registration and Disciplinary Comm'n of Illinois*, *infra* note 78. For a contemporary discussion of commercial speech developments in judicial, legislative, and regulatory venues see also Gartner, Michael G., *Advertising and the First Amendment*, (New York: Priority Press Publications, 1989).

Chapter 2

[14] *Valentine v. Chrestensen*, 316 U.S. 52 (1942).

[15] *Id.* at 53.

[16] *Id.* at 54.

[17] *Id.* at 55.

[18] *Cammarano v. U.S.*, 358 U.S. 498, 514 (1959)(Douglas, J., concurring).

[19] *Id.* at 513.

[20] *Pittsburgh Press Co. v. Pittsburgh Comm'n on Human Relations*, 413 U.S. 376 (1973).

[21] *Id.* at 385. A number of cases before the Court prior to 1973 touched on commercial speech questions. *See, for example, Head v. New Mexico Board of Examiners of Optometry*, 374 U.S. 424 (1963); *Banzhaf v. FCC*, 405 F.2d 1082 (D.C. Cir. 1968), *cert. denied*, 396 U.S. 842 (1969); *Rowan v. U.S. Post Office Dept.*, 300 F. Supp. 1036 (C.D. Cal. 1969), *aff'd*, 397 U.S. 728 (1970); *SEC v. Wall Street Transcript Corp.*, 422 F.2d 1371 (2d Cir. 1970), *cert. denied*, 398 U.S. 958 (1970); *Dun & Bradstreet, Inc. v. Grove*, 404 U.S. 898 (1971); *Capital Broadcasting Co. v. Mitchell*, 333 F. Supp. 582 (D. D.C. 1971), *aff'd*, 405 U.S. 1000 (1972); and *U.S. v. Hunter*, 459 F.2d 205 (4th Cir. 1972), *cert. denied*, 409 U.S. 934 (1972).

[22] *Bigelow v. Virginia*, 421 U.S. 809 (1975).

[23] *Id.* at 818.

[24] *Id.* at 812.

[25] *Id.* at 824.

[26] *Id.* at 824-825.

[27] *Id.* at 825.

[28] *New York Times Co. v. Sullivan*, 376 U.S. 254, 266 (1964).

[29] *See also*, other cases from the mid-1970s such as *Lehman v. City of Shaker Heights*, 418 U.S. 298 (1974); *Fur Information & Fashion Council, Inc. v. E.F. Timme & Son, Inc.*, 364 F. Supp. 16 (S.D.N.Y. 1973), *aff'd on other grounds*, 501 F. 2d 1048 (2d Cir. 1974), *cert. denied*, 419 U.S. 1022 (1974); *Rinaldi v. Village Voice, Inc.* ,47 A.D.2d 180, 365 N.Y.S. 2d 199, *cert. denied*, 423 U.S. 883 (1975); and *Terry v. California State Board of Pharmacy*, 395 F. Supp. 94 (N.D. Cal. 1975), *aff'd without opinion*, 426 U.S. 913 (1976).

[30] *Virginia State Board of Pharmacy v. Virginia Citizens Consumer Council, Inc.*, 425 U.S. 748 (1976).

[31] *Id.* at 760-761.

[32] *Id.* at 757.

[33] *Id.* at 756 (note omitted).

[34] *Lamont v. Postmaster General*, 381 U.S. 301 (1965).

[35] *Kleindienst v. Mandel*, 408 U.S. 753, 762-763 (1972).

[36] *Procunier v. Martinez*, 416 U.S. 396, 408-409 (1974).

[37] *Va. Pharmacy Board v. Va. Consumer Council*, *supra* note 30 at 763.

[38] *Id.* at 770.

[39] *Central Hudson Gas & Electric Corp. v. Public Service Comm'n of New York*, 447 U.S. 557 (1980).

[40] Commercial speech protection decreased in increments between *Virginia Pharmacy Board* in 1976 and *Central Hudson* in 1980. Compare *Linmark Associates, Inc. v. Township of Willingboro*, 431 U.S. 85 (1977) and *Carey v. Population Services International*, 431 U.S. 678 (1977) with *Friedman v. Rogers*, 440 U.S. 1 (1979) and *Century 21 Real Estate Corp. v. Nevada Real Estate Advisory Comm'n*, 448 F. Supp. 1237 (1978), *aff'd*, 440 U.S. 941 (1979). Also during this time the Court ruled that political (as opposed to commercial) speech by corporations was fully protected under the First Amendment. *See First National Bank of Boston v. Bellotti*, 435 U.S. 765 (1978).

[41] *Central Hudson v. Public Service Comm'n, supra* note 39 at 561.

[42] *Id.* at 562.

[43] *Id.* at 563.

[44] *Id.*

[45] *Id.* at 566.

[46] *Id.* at 569.

[47] *Id.* at 571 (note omitted). Other cases with commercial speech implications during the *Central Hudson* era included *Metromedia, Inc. v. City of San Diego*, 453 U.S. 490 (1981) (outdoor advertising signs); *Village of Hoffman Estates v. The Flipside, Hoffman Estates, Inc.*, 455 U.S. 489 (1982)(drug paraphernalia); *Bolger v. Youngs Drug Products Corp.*, 463 U.S. 60 (1983)(direct-mail ads for prophylactics); *City Council v. Taxpayers for Vincent*, 466 U.S. 789 (1984)(political posters); and *Dun & Bradstreet, Inc. v. Greenmoss Builders, Inc.*, 472 U.S. 749 (1985)(erroneous credit report).

[48] *Posadas de Puerto Rico Assoc's v. Tourism Co. of Puerto Rico*, 478 U.S. 328 (1986).

[49] *Id.* at 332.

[50] *Id.* at 337.

[51] *Id.* at 340.

[52] *Id.* at 341.

[53] *Id.*

[54] *Id.* at 343.

[55] *Id.* at 345-346.

[56] *Board of Trustees of the State Univ. of New York v. Fox*, 109 S. Ct. 3028 (1989).

[57] *Id.* at 3030.

[58] *Id.* at 3030, citing 841 F.2d 1207 (1988).

[59] *Id.* at 3031.

[60] *Id.* at 3032.

[61] *Id.* at 3032-3033.

[62] *Id.* at 3035.

[63] *Id.*

[64] *Id.* at 3038.

[65] *See Va. Pharmacy Board v. Va. Consumer Council, supra* note 30 (drugs); *Linmark Assoc's v. Willingboro, supra* note 40 (real estate); and *Carey v. Population Services, supra* note 40 (prophylactics).

[66] Kozinski, Alex and Banner, Stuart, "Who's afraid of commercial speech?" 76 *Virginia L. Rev.* 627, 630 (May 1990).

[67] *Bates v. State Bar of Arizona*, 433 U.S. 350 (1977).

[68] *Id.* at 379.

[69] *In re Primus*, 436 U.S. 412 (1978).

[70] *Ohralik v. Ohio State Bar Ass'n*, 436 U.S. 447 (1978).

[71] *In re R.M.J.*, 455 U.S. 191 (1982).

[72] *Id.* at 203.

[73] *Id.*

[74] *Zauderer v. Office of Disciplinary Counsel*, 471 U.S. 626 (1985).

[75] *Id.*

[76] *Shapero v. Kentucky Bar Ass'n*, 486 U.S. 466 (1988).

[77] *Id.*

[78] *Peel v. Attorney Registration and Disciplinary Comm'n of Illinois*, 110 S. Ct. 2281 (1990).

[79] *See also, Austin v. Michigan Chamber of Commerce*, 110 S. Ct. 1391 (1990). While generally regarded as a decision on campaign financing with implications for political speech, it narrowed the First Amendment protection afforded speech by corporations. An excellent outline of commercial speech cases, including many lower court decisions, is presented in DeVore, P. Cameron and Sack, Robert D., "Advertising and Commercial Speech," in Goodale, James C. (chmn.), *Communications Law 1990*, (New York: Practising Law Institute, 1990), at 7-422.

Chapter 3

[80] Smith, Craig R., *All Speech Is Created Equal*, (Long Beach, Cal.: Freedom of Expression Foundation, 1990), at 4.

[81] Report on the Virginia Resolutions, Jan. 1800, reprinted in Kurland, P. and Lerner R., eds., 5 *The Founders' Constitution* 122, 141, 145 (1987), cited in Kozinski and Banner, "Who's afraid of commercial speech?" *supra* note 66 at 632.

[82] Kozinski and Banner, "Who's afraid of commercial speech?" *supra* note 66 at 632.

[83] Bork, Robert H., "Neutral principles and some First Amendment problems," 47 *Indiana L. Journ.* 1, 22 (Fall 1971).

[84] *Id.*

[85] *Id.*

[86] A concise explication is offered by Burt Neuborne in "Commercial free speech in the marketplace of ideas," 41 *Rutgers L. Rev.* 719, 726-727 (1989).

[87] To quote the phrase used by Justice Brandeis in *Whitney v. California, infra.*

[88] *Whitney v. California*, 274 U.S. 357 (1927).

[89] Neuborne in "Commercial free speech in the marketplace of ideas," *supra* note 86 at 727.

[90] *Id.*

[91] *See, for example, Martin v. City of Struthers*, 319 U.S. 141 (1943)(proselytizing) and *Schad v. Borough of Mt. Ephraim*, 452 U.S. 61 (1981)(nude dancing).

[92] Bork, "Neutral principles and some First Amendment problems," *supra* note 83 at 29.

[93] *First National Bank of Boston v. Bellotti*, 435 U.S. 765 (1978).

[94] Baker, C. Edwin, "Commercial speech: A problem in the theory of freedom," 62 *Iowa L. Rev.* 1, 17 (1976).

[95] Neuborne in "Commercial free speech in the marketplace of ideas," *supra* note 86 at 728.

[96] Shiffrin, Steven, "The First Amendment and economic regulation: Away from a general theory of the First Amendment," 78 *Northwestern Univ. L. Rev.* 1212 (1984).

[97] Farber, Daniel A., "Commercial speech and First Amendment theory," 74 *Northwestern Univ. L. Rev.* 372, 399 (1979).

[98] Shiffrin, "The First Amendment and economic regulation: Away from a general theory of the First Amendment," *supra* note 96 at 1261.

[99] Bork, "Neutral principles and some First Amendment problems," *supra* note 83 at 21.

[100] *United States v. O'Brien*, 391 U.S. 367 (1968).

[101] *Id.* at 377.

[102] *Central Hudson v. Public Service Comm'n, supra* note 39 at 566.

[103] *S.U.N.Y. v. Fox, supra* note 56 at 3029.

[104] Kozinski and Banner, "Who's afraid of commercial speech?" *supra* note 66 at 631. Their notes 21-26 are included below as notes 105-110. Other types of speech are also subject to restriction. *See, for example, Chaplinsky v. New Hampshire*, 315 U.S. 568, 572 (1942) (fighting words); *Roth v. U.S.*, 354

U.S. 476, 481-485 (1957) and *Miller v. California*, 413 U.S. 15, 23 (1973) (obscenity); *Gertz v. Robert Welch, Inc.*, 418 U.S. 323 (1974) (libel); and *Brandenburg v. Ohio*, 395 U.S. 444 (1969) (incitement).

[105] *See Metromedia, Inc. v. City of San Diego*, 453 U.S. 490 (1981).

[106] *See San Francisco Arts & Athletics, Inc. v. United States Olympic Comm.*, 483 U.S. 522 (1987).

[107] *See Bolger v. Youngs Drug Prods. Corp.*, 463 U.S. 60 (1983).

[108] *See Posadas de P.R. Assocs. v. Tourism Co.*, 478 U.S. 328 (1986).

[109] *See Riley v. National Fed'n of the Blind*, 108 S. Ct. 2667 (1988).

[110] *See Board of Trustees of the State Univ. of N.Y. v. Fox*, 109 S. Ct. 3028 (1989).

Chapter 4

[111] *Valentine v. Chrestensen*, *supra* note 14.

[112] *Cammarano v. U.S.*, *supra* note 18.

[113] *Pittsburgh Press v. Human Rel. Comm'n*, *supra* note 20.

[114] *Id.* at 385.

[115] *Central Hudson v. Public Service Comm'n*, *supra* note 39 at 561.

[116] *Va. Pharmacy Board v. Va. Consumer Council*, *supra* note 30 at 762.

[117] *Bates v. State Bar of Arizona*, *supra* note 67 at 364.

[118] *New York Times Co. v. Sullivan*, *supra* note 28 at 266.

[119] *Id.*

[120] *Va. Pharmacy Bd. v. Va. Consumer Council*, *supra* note 30 at 761.

[121] *Id.* at 762, citing *NLRB v. Gissel Packing Co.*, 395 U.S. 575, 617-618 (1969); *NLRB v. Virginia Electric & Power Co.*, 314 U.S. 469, 477 (1941); *AFL v. Swing*, 312 U.S. 321, 325-326 (1941); and *Thornhill v. Alabama*, 310 U.S. 88, 102 (1940).

[122] *S.U.N.Y. v. Fox*, *supra* note 56 at 3036.

[123] *First National Bank of Boston v. Bellotti, supra* note 93.

[124] *Id.* at 784.

[125] *Valentine v. Chrestensen, supra* note 14 at 55.

[126] *Bigelow v. Virginia, supra* note 22 at 822 (note omitted).

[127] *Bolger v. Youngs Drug Prods. Corp., supra* note 107.

[128] *Nat. Comm'n on Egg Nutrition v. FTC*, 570 F.2d 157 (7th Cir. 1977), *cert. denied*, 439 U.S. 821 (1978).

[129] *Id.* at 163.

[130] *In re R.J. Reynolds Tobacco Co.*, [1983-1987 Transfer Binder] Trade Reg. Rep. (CCH) ¶22,385, at 23,467 (Aug. 6, 1986), *rev'd*, Trade Reg. Rep. (CCH) ¶22,522, at 22,180 (Apr. 11, 1988), *stay denied*, Trade Reg. Rep. (CCH) ¶22,549, at 22,231 (June 3, 1988).

[131] *See, for example*, Kozinski and Banner, "Who's afraid of commercial speech?" *supra* note 66 at 635-648.

[132] *Va. Pharmacy Bd. v. Va. Consumer Council, supra* note 30 at 771-772 (n. 24).

[133] *Id.* at 772.

[134] Farber, "Commercial speech and First Amendment theory," *supra* note 97 at 389.

[135] *Id.* at 387.

[136] *Id.* at 389.

Chapter 5

[137] *Va. Pharmacy Bd. v. Va. Consumer Council, supra* note 30 at 763.

[138] *Director, Aaron*, "The parity of the economic market place," 7 *J.L. & Econ.* 1, 6 (1964), cited in Kozinski and Banner, *supra* note 66 at 652.

[139] *Bates v. State Bar of Arizona, supra* note 67 at 364. *See also FTC v. Procter & Gamble Co.*, 386 U.S. 568, 603-604 (1967) (Harlan, J., concurring).

[140] *See, for example, Martin v. Struthers*, 319 U.S. 141, 143 (1943); *Thomas v. Collins*, 323 U.S. 516, 534 (1945); and *Associated Press v. U.S.* 326 U.S. 1, 20 (1945).

[141] *Kleindienst v. Mandel*, 408 U.S. 753, 762-763 (1972).

[142] *Red Lion Broadcasting Co., Inc. v. FCC*, 395 U.S. 367, 390 (1969).

[143] *Va. Pharmacy Bd. v. Va. Consumer Council, supra* note 30 at 756, 757.

[144] *Lamont v. Postmaster General*, 381 U.S. 301 (1965).

[145] *Procunier v. Martinez*, 416 U.S. 396 (1974).

[146] Kozinski and Banner, "Who's afraid of commercial speech?" *supra* note 66 at 651.

[147] A prescription metaphor seems appropriate here to remind us of *Virginia Pharmacy Board*, the high point of commercial speech protection.

[148] *Pittsburgh Press v. Human Rel. Comm'n, supra* note 20 at 402 (Stewart, J., dissenting).

[149] *Elrod v. Burns*, 427 U.S. 347, 373 (1976).

[150] *Statement of Chairman James C. Miller III, Policy Statement Regarding Advertising Substantiation Program*, July 27, 1984, at 3.

[151] Crawford, Carol, "Remarks before the American Advertising Federation," Dec. 4, 1984, at 19-20.

Index

Richard T. Kaplar is Vice President of The Media Institute in Washington, D.C. He has written, edited, or produced over 30 books and monographs on a variety of communications topics. He is the editor of *Beyond the Courtroom: Alternatives for Resolving Press Disputes*, and is the author of *The Financial Interest and Syndication Rules: Prime Time for Repeal*.

Harvey L. Zuckman is Director of the Institute for Communications Law Studies at the Catholic University of America in Washington, D.C. A professor of law at the University's Columbus School of Law, he teaches torts and conducts a research seminar on First Amendment problems of the media. Prof. Zuckman has written extensively in legal journals on First Amendment and media law subjects, has co-authored *Mass Communications Law*, a student text now in its third edition, and is a former editor of the American Bar Association's newsletter *Communications Lawyer*. The Institute for Communications Law Studies provides numerous courses and internships for a select group of law students who wish to pursue careers in the field of communications law.

The Media Institute is a nonprofit, tax-exempt research foundation supported by a wide range of foundations, corporations, associations, and individuals. The Institute publishes studies, conducts conferences, and sponsors other programs on a host of communications policy issues. Through its First Amendment Center, the Institute has filed numerous court briefs and comments with regulatory agencies advocating full First Amendment rights for all types of speakers—individual, media, and corporate. To support the work of the Institute, or for further information, please contact Patrick D. Maines, President, The Media Institute, 3017 M Street, N.W., Washington, D.C. 20007.

Advertising Rights: The Neglected Freedom was produced by David P. Taggart. Sharon Anthony provided editorial assistance and compiled the index.